NOT ONLY PEACE

Not Only Peace

*Christian Realism and the Conflicts
of the Twentieth Century*

ALAN R. BOOTH

SCM PRESS LTD
BLOOMSBURY STREET LONDON

by the same author
Christians and Power Politics

First published 1967
© *SCM Press Ltd 1967*
Printed in Great Britain by
Northumberland Press Limited
Gateshead

CONTENTS

Introduction		7
1	WHY WARS?	15
2	THE DANGERS OF MORALISING	37
3	THE REALISM OF THE BIBLE	54
4	CHRISTIANITY AND POWER	71
5	'PROGRESSIVE' GOVERNMENT	82
6	THE REALISTIC HOPE	97
7	INSTITUTIONS OF PEACE	111
8	TRUE RELIGION IN THE POLITICAL REALM	126
	Index	141

5

INTRODUCTION

PICASSO IS REPUTED to have insisted that he painted his works of art to prevent himself biting his nails. This book lays no claim to be such a work of art, but at least it has similar origins. For anyone who allows himself to get deeply involved in the passionate conflicts between and within nations is constantly driven to the utmost limits of frustration by the experience that such conflicts are so difficult to discuss with any degree of rationality. The reason for this is in part that the protagonists all start from different premises, prejudices and assumptions. These in turn are no doubt subject to rational debate—if ever there were a moment when the pressure for immediate decisions relaxed sufficiently to allow the debate to proceed. But at such a moment of *détente* the normal man much prefers to talk about something else. The whole object of writing this particular kind of book is to entice some people to consider the larger questions of assumptions and premises before we find ourselves once more in furious combat, dialectical or physical, on an issue over which we have completely lost rational contact with each other.

This means, of course, that this book is designed to induce conversation rather than to conclude it. But that does not imply that the author is some sort of uncommitted Jove regarding with detached and sceptical amusement the foolish attempts of mortals to recognise meaning and value in the human struggle. So at the outset he should indicate his standpoint. First of all the book is explicitly written from a position of commitment to the Christian faith. But I am not at all happy about the conclusions that many of my Christian contemporaries draw from this faith. Those who are themselves directly occupied in handling political realities tend too often to think that the Christian faith is like a nice fairy story which is read to you at the end of a

7

troublesome and disturbing day to help you to go to sleep. It represents unattainable ideals which one needs to contemplate at least to disperse complacencies and stimulate effort, but fundamentally it speaks of a world which is not this one. I respect those who draw strength and inspiration from such a view of the matter, and do not for a moment doubt that its effect is generally beneficent. I simply doubt whether it has much connexion with the real Christian tradition, or is not at best an amalgam of bits of various kinds of Greek philosophy, Platonism and Stoicism, with a few selected Bible references and a good dose of the English public school tradition—admirable indeed, but sailing under a false flag.

But further, I feel with many another the compelling need to abandon the convenient theological short-hand in which Christians have been accustomed to communicate with each other in days when the generality of Western mankind shared a common language about religion. Most of mankind is now seen to be other than Western, to be outside the Christian orbit, or (even if Western) no longer able to give any real meaning to those old-fashioned short-hand words about God, incarnation, atonement and the rest which provided the vocabulary of a very powerful but confined little clique of the human race. So much is this the case, that we have now to work out a new vocabulary to convey what we intend to say to each other. One of the most rewarding and demanding ways of doing this is to talk profoundly to each other about some important matter of common concern—such as international peace. If the reader is aware of the writer's groans as he tries to avoid falling back into language that has become meaningless, an apology in advance is sincerely tended. But the reason, I hope, will be respected. It is a desire not to talk simply to the 'converted' but to find the way to participation in a general human discussion in which it is possible for the riches of the Christian faith to be presented in a form that has some general intellectual persuasiveness today.

Then again there are those who think, not without good reason, that if you bring the Christian faith into the argument you bring in the figure of the school-master, of the 'disapproving church', of the men of earnest mien constantly going on about moral issues. It is not that we would not concede the importance

of some kind of loyalty to what is right and some kind of dis-
association from what is wrong. But in part our sense of weariness with the protests of such people stems from the feeling that
you cannot reach real and sensible decisions simply on such a
basis—that somehow life demands of us a more complex and
sensitive response than the apparent legalism of our critics provides. But I have a particular preoccupation in this field. We all
perceive that as a race we are entering upon a process of rapid
change unprecedented in history, both in scope and speed. Our
discovery of the means to master nature presents us with such a
novel range of choices and decisions that old examples and principles no longer fit our present problems. The intellectual
struggles within the ranks of Christian moralists to come to
terms with birth-control reveal the dilemma. But there are a lot
more conundrums of the same sort on the way. What is needed
now is not loyalty to past recognition of the good enshrined in a
set of eternal principles so much as a capacity for moral creativity. How you venture on such an enterprise, what you can
legitimately take with you, are questions not to be answered in
the abstract but in an actual attempt to resolve problems—such
as those in the international field.

That is one sense in which I have attempted to drop a book
down into the gap between two sets of contenders—in this case
between those who would call themselves Christians on the one
hand, and those who are deeply committed to the human enterprise but without religious affiliation on the other. There is
another set of twins too which I have had in mind: those who
experience life in terms of action and decision and those who do
so in terms of thought and reflection. 'After all' Winston
Churchill once wrote, 'a man's life must be nailed to the cross
either of thought or of action.'[1] But there is an estrangement
between the two types of people which is not so necessary. The
man of action can be driven mad by the criticism of one whom
he regards as an irresponsible commentator. The commentator
has not the discipline of having to live with the results of the
policies he recommends; he does not need to go through the
labour of trying to make them work; he can in a few months

---

[1] *My Early Life*, p. 111.

happily reverse his position and start advocating something quite different. In short he knows nothing of the burden, at once exhilarating and educative, of committing men and societies to courses of action the end of which cannot be accurately foreseen but for which one will be held publicly responsible. That is the feeling in the minds of many men of action about 'the amateur', 'the spectator', 'the commentator'. They half-envy the possibility of preserving a high moral position; they half-despise those who know nothing of the manly guilt of making any decision.

The other side is no less articulate. They see not simply men of action but men who enjoy power. They are not greatly deceived by protests of the burdens undertaken and responsibilities carried, for they think the protesters have chosen their own role and like it. They perceive how easily men who make decisions are led to make those decisions which are convenient to themselves, their group or their country, and how necessary is the criticism of people less involved, with more time and perhaps ability for reaching objective, critical appraisals. Only such criticism, they believe, will explore all the possibilities of a situation and avert the danger that we are committed to a self-justifying chain of consequences which proves disastrous in the end.

The first group—the men of action—will demand of this book that it be brief, clear and practical. The second will ask that, however long, it will develop a sound intellectual critique, which cannot be gainsaid, of the current assumptions of our society, even if it leaves it a little uncertain what the consequences for practical policy might be. Anyone who tries to speak to both sides is no doubt foolhardy for he cannot readily please both. I have the impression that this present book may please neither, and once again aim to disarm criticism by offering apology. I have deliberately eschewed practical policy proposals for a variety of reasons. The first is simply that the aim has been to clear up the context rather than the details of policies. But I have avoided even the possibility of illustration of a general point by a consideration of how it might work out in terms of policy for another reason—that such illustration goes so quickly out of date. This debate on policies is the substance of the daily press, the weekly review and even of the specialist quarterly. A book had better keep to subjects less ephemeral. There are, scattered throughout, a number of launching pads for policies which the discerning intelligence will identify, but no attempt has been made to design the actual missiles. I would have to allow that there is also here a reflection of the desire to find an alternative to biting my nails. If one's daily life is much occupied in questions of details of policy, the only relief to be found lies in a deliberate search for another way of looking at the problems.

But I think I may claim that at least I have dealt briefly with a huge subject, and here I count on men of action to defend me from the others, who will hurl the criticism that such brevity is a major fault. Why are not the arguments fully developed? Why throw out a tantalising hint and then leave the reader to pursue it alone through the forest of his own mind? I could excuse myself by saying that I have at least gone to a little trouble to provide clues in the notes for those who want company in the forest; that I have there suggested where a position briefly described can be seen more fully detailed and defended. I could point out that a book designed for this particular gap fails in its purpose if it becomes a tome. But to be honest the determining factor lies in a sense that the things I want to convey will need, perhaps more than argumentation, something which I would call recognition—and the process of recognition may be hindered rather than helped if blanketed by a heavy burden of intellectual apparatus. Am I right to imagine that the truths of greatest consequence, while they must be intellectually defensible, are reached and cleaved to in a response more totally involving ourselves, our mind, imagination and will? If that is so there is still a case for some method equivalent to speaking in parables.

What therefore I have attempted is what I have described—a view. A fairly wide-ranging view because the proportions and significance of much of the detail is determined by the complete whole. Any one detail could perhaps occupy a book in itself, and all I can do is to indicate where such a treatment might be found, and then hurry on to the rest of the scene. Parts of the finished work are as unsatisfactory to me as they are likely to prove to some readers, and I conclude that they represent the in-built limitations of the present author rather than necessary obscurities in the subject. But the aim of the work will be achieved if it directs attention to the larger debate within which the heated controversies of international politics may be better understood and therefore the temptations to war even slightly abated.

The underlying theme of the book is peace. This is an already somewhat dusty subject, and it is commonly recognised that it takes about twenty years from one major war for conditions to arise which permit the serious contemplation of organising the next. The twenty years are up and so we see the odd spectacle of those who denounced their neighbours in the past by accusing them of being too militaristic now devoting their energies with some eagerness to the job of seeing that they are on the right side in the next experiments in war. If we refuse to accept that peace is something which cannot be sustained for half a lifetime at the least, we must view this anticipated and unwelcome evolution of men's passions with disquiet. Peace is still important, even while it is still true that it cannot be had by simply abandoning weapons. What are the roads towards it? What are the main threats to it? Can one understand our human predicament more deeply so that one can see more sharply what to avoid to escape the delusions of bellicosity? These are the questions to which this book is addressed.

I do not imagine that there is here anything more original than the bringing together of the thoughts of better minds than mine in a new relation to each other. For that reason I ought to acknowledge that at every stage I am in someone else's debt. But in particular I owe a debt to those with whom I am associated in the Commission of the Churches on International Affairs for the opportunity to participate in continuing discussion and action in pursuit of international peace and justice. My colleagues in the Secretariat of the Commission have been patient of those lapses of punctuality or efficiency arising from the attempt to write a book in the interstices of the working week. But their patience and forebearance implies in no sense that they are identified with my views or opinions, nor that the Commission which I serve gives or withholds any endorsement of what I have written. This naturally applies equally to our parent body, the World Council of Churches, at whose conferences on these matters I have learnt so much and met such stimulating people. The liberty I have sought to frame an argument and present it publicly has been readily accorded as being part of the ecumenical tradition we all try to serve. But it can be indulged only if it is made clear beyond shadow of doubt that no-one but myself is responsible for what I have written.

It is a charming courtesy to express at this point one's indebtedness to one's wife for her encouragement, for her help perhaps in typing the manuscript, correcting the proofs or compiling an index. I typed the manuscript myself and corrected the proofs. My wife did something quite different. By that telepathy which works without words, she directed me at each stage of the writing to material in books and articles which critically advanced or illuminated my own thought, and gave what value there may be to the chapters which follow. I am not clear how this happened. For a long time I was unable or unwilling to explain the scheme and structure of the book, but this proved no obstacle to her. With precision and insight, in the course of her own work, she identified just those sources of material that set me off again at the typewriter. Thus to speak of her encouragement is a considerable understatement. The reader must judge for himself whether or not she was well advised.

I

WHY WARS?

MAJOR WAR IS totally irrational in the nuclear age—the observation is a familiar one which yet fails to provide the reassurance expected of it. We are not at all certain just how far human affairs are in fact controlled by rationality. Indeed it is probably true that war has never been a very rational way of pursuing the future welfare of mankind. The advent of nuclear weapons has merely heavily underlined a truism of history. Yet wars have happened, and go on happening in circumstances which persuade the participants either that they have no alternative or that in this particular case the general rule does not apply.

This ominous reflection has for centuries forced thinking men and women to seek a root cause which could be isolated and suppressed. Three main theories of the origins of warfare have had their adherents, and all three have their particular modern versions. It is the purpose of this chapter to look briefly at each in turn and then to consider in greater detail a fourth which belongs peculiarly to the age of modern educated 'democratic' societies, living in an era of secularism with the resources of modern technology, nuclear fission in particular, at its disposal.[1]

The first root is that to which the charter of UNESCO refers: 'Wars begin in the minds of men'. What is it about men's minds that condemns us to this absurd recurrent violence? It is scarcely enough to say that we are wicked, for this merely adds a moral dimension to the denunciation under which we already stand

---

[1] The pattern, and some considerable part of the material in this chapter are derived from Kenneth N. Waltz, *Man, the State and War: a Theoretical Analysis* (New York: Columbia University Press, 1959). It will be seen that the whole book is built on a frame originally developed by Waltz.

without clarifying it. The behavioural scientists point out that there are societies where war is unknown. It is therefore reasonable to assume that, given different cultural patterns and social organisation, we could discover a way of life which no longer found war in the least interesting or tempting. Some of us may know households where, following this kind of reasoning, the children are not allowed to play with toy soldiers in the hope that the militaristic imagination can be exorcized. In the same vein, men have sought less harmful outlets for our 'aggressive instincts', and believed that if they could be taken care of in other ways, men would not burst out from time to time in a frenzy of bellicosity. Psychologists have made specific analysis of the typical faults of character in leading statesmen which tend to warp their judgement in the direction of unreasonable self-assertion and the desire to impose their wills on others, and have even suggested a psychological screening system to reject unsuitable types.

Why is it that this approach immediately strikes us as unreal? It is obviously not because the improvement of human character or the correction of our emotional disturbances is of itself an unimportant or irrelevant undertaking. It is partly because it seems so blissfully unaware of the time factor. Dr Margaret Mead, who has herself ventured in this field as an eminent anthropologist, has, in her later years, written as though she believed we could purposively settle down to creating a brand new culture, drawing from all available resources of cultural experience, in which the futility of war would never be questioned. But in her great work *Coming of Age in Samoa* she fully recognised that far-reaching changes in a culture 'are the work of time, a work in which each individual plays an unconscious and inconsiderable part'. This is the instinctive perception of those of us less technically equipped than she is, who fear that the prescription will not yet have cured the patient long after we are all dead.

But there is another reason. It is one which indicates the grim connexion between man's creativity and his destructiveness. For it is the very civilisation which, with supreme self-confidence, has asserted the human capacity to master his environment which has also proved capable of the most appalling warfare. No doubt the connexion is in part due to the fact that scientific mastery necessarily produced massively destructive weapons. But there is more to it than that. The type of mind which conceives of the task of mastering its environment will also set about mastering other human beings who form a significant part of that environment. Moreover it is a type of mind capable of great imaginative systems of thought with which to interpret human history and experience—systems which it will hold the more dear as giving purpose and meaning to human existence. An opposing culture which threatens, not only one's frontiers or physical welfare, but far more fundamentally one's understanding of existence, appears to be something to be resisted with every nerve and sinew one can muster.

Our suspicion of this formula for tackling the roots of warfare is therefore compounded of at least two elements: doubt about its time-scale, and doubt whether the proposed culture and human type would not prove to be so emasculated as to take from life one of its most valued features and risk making life meaningless. We shall return to this last aspect of the question later in this chapter. For the moment it is perhaps enough to ask whether the type of man conjured up by the behavioural scientists as admirable would not prove in fact to be nothing more remarkable than 'harmless'; whether the screened statesman would not turn out to be a man who would much rather be playing chamber music than running a nation; and whether there is not required in those who create and lead and adventure a peculiar (and not necessarily malevolent) quality which appears to be closely related to romantic brigandage.

'Wars begin in the minds of men', and UNESCO, in asserting this, did not have primarily in view the task of emotional adjustment but rather the significance of education and the spread of knowledge. What makes men fight each other is their failure to perceive their common nature or interest. So it becomes necessary to apply reason to prejudice, for instance by scientific verification of our common human nature in contradiction to the assertions of racialist propagandists. We must also spread true information to dissipate the monstrous caricatures we harbour of each other, and learn to appreciate and understand other cultures and traditions than our own. All of which is profoundly true, and made the easier by modern means of travel and methods of communication; Telstar, Eurovision and the rest. While the process of getting acquainted has certainly begun on a scale never before conceivable, yet there remains a limitless field to be explored. Looking at the matter from a European angle, the task of understanding China and its ancient civilisation on the one hand, and Africa with its highly personalised and un-complex responses on the other, has scarcely begun.

But it is evidently an oversimplification to imagine that the process is a simple matter of replacing emotional reactions by objective and reasonable information. In the first place knowing other people is an altogether different matter from knowing about them or about things. It depends in large measure on the extent to which the other person wishes to reveal and interpret himself to me. This in turn is profoundly emotionally con-ditioned, depending on whether he thinks I am trustworthy or will use what I know of him to his detriment; and also on whether he cares enough about the encounter to go to the trouble of interpretation. It has been remarked that whereas the African, living traditionally a geographically spacious existence, within the securities of tribal life, tends to reveal his emotions with enviable spontaneity within his accustomed environment, the really ancient civilisations of men, from the Eastern Med-iterranean eastwards, have learnt a greater caution from their encounter with larger communities and more frequent strangers. They hide their feelings with care, knowing how easy it is for men to take advantage of one another once they observe each other's emotional vulnerabilities.

The other fundamental obstacle to the process of mutual understanding has already been hinted at—to discover another culture is not necessarily to like it. What is worse, it may appear on closer acquaintance to possess elements which seem to threaten our own most highly valued perceptions of the good. Milner is recorded as remarking to his chief, Sir Evelyn Baring, shortly after arriving to serve under him in Egypt, that he hoped international hatred and suspicion could be reduced by getting nations 'to understand one another better'. There is perhaps a weariness of experience in Sir Evelyn's reply: 'I'm afraid, my dear Milner, that the better they understand one another the

more they will hate one another.'[2] We must look critically at
the assumption, common to liberal thought in a number of
different fields, that there is in our human situation a natural
harmony—of aspiration, interest or affection—if only we are
reasonable enough to take the trouble to discover it. To accept
the assumption unexamined may be defended as indicating a
positive and forward-looking attitude to life. But it may equally
be the sign of a timid and unserious mind. For it would be hard
to demonstrate objectively from either present experience or history that the proposition of essential harmony is true. Is it really
impossible that men should disagree with one another about the
most fundamental considerations of life? Were all the terrible
wars of religion and ideology furious quarrels over a simple misunderstanding? Or, as Marxist analysis would have it, were they
conflicts of economic interest, clothed in a bizarre fancy dress? It
is comfortable to fall back into some sort of basic relativism
whereby all human value-judgements are seen as lacking any
objective reality, so that there is no ultimate justification for falling out with each other about them. The passivities of certain
oriental religions reflect the search for such a *modus vivendi*, and
it scarcely behoves Christians to despise too hastily what is there
affirmed in view of the terrible human suffering which has
accompanied a more aggressively dogmatic creed. Yet when all
our arrogant assertiveness has been properly brought low, we
may still believe that there is for us men a more coherent
rationale of existence than that which can be supplied by an
eternal question mark. We may go further and ask if the great
contemporary enterprise of attempting to free mankind at last
from the slavery of poverty, ignorance and disease can in fact be
pursued effectively in a cultural environment so determinedly
doubtful of the validity of any values. There are strong reasons
for believing that the two cannot co-exist, and that if traditional
values are discarded men will find it necessary to invent and believe in new ones. And there is no reason to assume that men will
necessarily agree with each other as to what these values are.

There is another possible basis for the assumption that it is
open to men to find a deep agreement about what makes life
worth living. This is the conviction that there exists a funda-

[2] F. S. Oliver, *The Endless Adventure*, vol. iii, p 177 n.

mental reality responding to the very nature of the human species, of which we can learn more together, and thereby draw nearer each other. This can be no more than an act of faith, although serious and reasonable investigation will show it to be a coherent view. But it is an act of faith to be distinguished relentlessly from all easy optimisms, in so far as it involves a personal commitment of limitless scope.

At this stage of the argument it is not proposed to pursue further these glimpses of what it means to say that wars begin in the minds of men. The intention is simply to note the limitations we must accept on the possibility that war can in practice be eradicated by some conceivable manipulation of the factors conditioning human thought. In noting the limitations, we are not, of course, intending to suggest that the enlargement of human understanding, the recognition of psychological weaknesses, and the nurture of the virtues of tolerance and humility make no great contribution to the peace of the world. All that is asserted is that, of themselves, they do not offer mankind a certain hope of escape from the scourge of war. It will be the business of a later chapter to examine in greater detail the contribution which moral purpose brings to the task of ordering international relations.

The second place where men have sought the root-cause of war is in the character of societies themselves, an analysis with which we are well familiar when we hear the appellation 'peace-loving states'. The argument runs as follows. It is evidently irrational, and far from being in the interest of the ordinary man, that armies should hurl themselves upon each other and upon the citizenry of opponents. The reason why such disasters occur is either that people are made the playthings of despots (who contrive to emerge themselves unscathed from the destruction), or there are in societies strains and contradictions which can find relief only in external adventures. In either case the seeds of war are to be found in the internal structure of the state itself, and so the way to peace is to be sought by reforming the social and political patterns within nations. Nowadays it is the second of the two forms of this argument which has the most frequent currency. Self-determination plus socialism is the recipe for contentment—and therefore for peace. Imperialism plus capitalism provide the ingredients for a war-monger. But there is a respectable history, too, for the earlier version in eighteenth and nineteenth century European political thought.

People are made the playthings of despots, who themselves are moved by vanity and foolish dreams of grandeur. So wars are made. This is the argument which led men to believe that once political power was effectively derived from the ordinary people, the common man, war would no longer be acceptable as a means of pursuing rational objectives. So Thomas Paine, in *The Rights of Man*, thought of the consequences of the French Revolution in 1791: 'Monarchical sovereignty, the enemy of mankind, and the source of misery, is abolished; and sovereignty itself is restored to its natural and original place, the nation. Were this the case throughout Europe, the cause of war would be taken away.' The sentiments of the generality of men being strongly against war, what was required was the means to make such sentiments effective in the control of national policies. Absolute power relieves the ruler of having to pay attention to such popular sentiments, so that he is free to pursue his wayward course. 'If any man possesses absolute power over the rest of the community, he is set free from all dependence upon their sentiments,' wrote James Mill in his essay on 'Law of Nations', and thus the force of pacific public opinion was unable to exercise its beneficial influence.

This may sound like the echo of a different age, until we reflect how it continues to influence the world's debate on the road to peace. The emphasis it places on the natural pacific tendency of ordinary men and women is heard again and again in the utterances of voluntary organisations within the peace movement. Mothers seek to create an international organisation amongst themselves, believing that the sources of conflict are wholly alien to their natural interest. Artists in various fields come together to fight the trend towards warfare on the assumption that the forces of hostility could find no echo in their own preoccupations. It is interesting also to observe the weight attributed by this type of thinking to the power of public opinion. Let men's voices be heard, compel the rulers to attend to the universal cry, and the danger is over. Something of this type of thinking can be found here and there in the ideas surrounding the true function of the United Nations. It is by no means a spent force in men's minds today.

Nor should it be. The perception that despotism is apt to be warlike is sound. There are several reasons. A man who is capable of bringing a whole society under his command is not likely to stop there. The natural vanities of our nature are greatly nourished by absolute power, and they join with the necessity to maintain an image of invincibility to urge aggressive policies. On the other hand, quite apart from any ascription of virtue, the electorate of a democracy is very slow to expose itself to the costs and risks of warfare—costs and risks which it will have to meet itself directly. Martial glory is a romantic prize perhaps for the man who can imagine himself at the head of the parade, but it looks like an expensive luxury to the average tax-payer. So it is that the business of steeling a democracy for war becomes daunting for a Churchill or a Roosevelt when they believe that the ultimate safety of the nation can be assured only by a readiness to fight.

There can be little argument to contradict the thesis that democracies are slow to arm, as a general rule. Unfortunately this is only half the picture. The other half concerns what happens once such societies have been persuaded, or have persuaded themselves, that war must be undertaken. The only terms on which the great majority of a nation will believe the perils of war worth risking are that a matter of quite fundamental human consequence is at stake. Thus Mazzini, seeking British aid against France in his campaign for Italian freedom, justified a warlike policy:

> War, with the scope of solving once for all the ancient problem whether Man is to remain a passive slave trodden underfoot by organised brute-force, or to become a free agent, responsible for his actions before God and his fellow men.... War, in the noble intention of restoring Truth and Justice, and of arresting Tyranny in her inhuman career, of rendering the Nations free and happy, and causing God to smile upon them benignantly, of crowning political and religious liberty....[3]

[3] Mazzini, *Selected Writings*, ed. Gangulee, p. 11. Written in 1853.

War, it might be said, to make the world safe for democracy. Only in some such perspective is it possible to galvanise a whole nation to take up arms. 'Either war is a crusade, or it is a crime' said R. H. Tawney, and our modern experience might lead us to add that, as a crusade, it can become the most monstrous crime of all. For the very moral fervour which is thus aroused makes it almost impossible to retain moral control over the military operations themselves. The enormity of the sin of the opponent, which alone justifies so dreadful a retort as war, places him beyond the pale of humane considerations if thereby his unconditional surrender should be either prejudiced or postponed.

The doctrine that war springs from the distorted social and political structure of individual states, and in particular that democracies, in contrast with despotisms, are 'peace loving', is therefore subject to serious qualification. It might be nearer the truth to say that democracies are slower to initiate war but apt to be more ruthless in pursuing it and relentless about the conditions on which they will terminate it. Moreover the thesis itself takes on a different aspect in the nuclear age. For modern weapons render obsolete much of the preconceptions on which the thesis was based. On the one hand, the conception of a people under arms, a citizen army, gives way to highly specialised military cadres, operating machines outside the appreciation of any but the expert. And on the other hand, it is scarcely thinkable that large-scale war can continue for any length of time, and that the people as a whole experience total mobilisation such as happened in the two Great Wars. The extent therefore to which the ordinary man can control hostilities through the exercise of his political power has been seriously reduced; and at the same time the degree to which he is expected to co-operate, other than as a victim, is equally minimised.

A much more sophisticated version of this analysis, which seeks the basic cause of war in the internal structure of states, derives from Marxism. In this view, there are two contradictions in capitalist societies which inevitably lead the ruling class to war. In the first place the productive system itself is built upon a form of latent warfare—between those who own the means of production and those employed to work it on the terms of the owners, such an exploitative system has to be prepared to suppress, from any quarter, the natural resentments and resistances which it provokes. Moreover, since the wealth distributed to the workers is always less than what they produce, it becomes necessary constantly to find new markets and new consumers for the surplus. These can be secured only by colonial conquest.

Before pulling to shreds such an understanding of our condition, it is important that those of us in the target area of the criticism recognise valid aspects of it. To begin with it is only fair to recall that the theory was built up not out of bitter hostility to any particular nation or race, but in reaction to the inhuman conditions in which men were compelled to live in the Britain of the Industrial Revolution. Basically it was a reaction of humanity. But equally important, it was the first sustained attempt to seek a cure for desperate ills of an industrial society, not by the blind assaults of resentful passion but by the application of scientific methods of analysis to social structures. It is not surprising that the first shot should not be in the centre of the target. But it has drawn attention for all time to the role of economic power within society, and to the fact that political appearances can disguise the fact that the place where crucial decisions affecting peace and war are taken may not be the place where they ought to be taken according to the constitution of a nation. It was President Eisenhower, no great disciple of Karl Marx, who warned his country as he laid down his presidential office of the danger of a military-industrial complex in the nation over which it was difficult for the government (representing the community interest as a whole) to gain control. But it must also be remembered that the man deputed by President Kennedy to assert that control, and who did it with outstanding success, was none other than a product of the capitalist system at its most characteristic—the President of the Ford Motor Corporation, Mr Robert McNamara, Secretary of Defence. The truth is, of course, that modern 'capitalist states' have gone a long way towards harnessing crude economic forces to the more general interest, and to fixing limits to the free exercise of economic power.

In the opposite camp, recent years have shown that 'socialist' systems of government do not inevitably find it easy to get along with each other. It used to be asserted that between a socialist

France and a socialist Germany there could be no problem of Alsace-Lorraine. The governments of France and Germany which first resolved the painful problem of the Saar together and then went on, in co-operation with other Europeans, to seek to bury for ever their rivalry in a single Economic Community, could not be considered classical specimens of socialism. And meanwhile Russia's conflict with Albania and Yugoslavia, and its much more significant controversy with Mao's China, show that interests may conflict very seriously even when ideologies seem to coincide.

Doubt is therefore thrown on the efficacy of this method of analysing the causes of war as a means of discovering the road to peace. Indeed the situation is even worse than that. For it may be contended that those who believe war to be caused by the inner faults of a state's social structure have a reasonable ground for doing their best to alter such states, if necessary by force. We are familiar with the reservation currently made by Russia concerning her devotion to peace—that her repugnance to war does not extend to 'wars of liberation', that is, wars directed to curing the interior diseases of states. But it is not always recalled that her reservation has been echoed on the Western side, in its 'war to end War,' or on the many occasions when men have asserted that peace may not be bought at the expense of justice.

It is possible to draw certain conclusion from this consideration of the effect of a state's internal social structure on its war-making proclivity. The more the community at large is involved in the political decisions determining foreign policy, the more brakes will operate on hasty aggressive decisions. On the other hand, once such a community is convinced that it is threatened by a state with a different ideological or political outlook, it will be hard to divert it from a war to the limit. The delicacies and refinements of diplomacy are quickly overwhelmed in the thunder of popular fear and bellicosity. Moreover, there is, as far as we know, no system of government and social organisation which, if adopted by various states, would of itself preclude the possibility of conflict. There continues to be a selfhood of nations or states which, whatever ideology or social organisation they profess allegiance to, seems to make it inevitable that there will be competition of interests between such selves, and therefore that there will always be the possibility that such competition will be pursued in open conflict. The very existence of international structures involves not only the possibility of co-operative policies but also the vigorous pursuit of influence to ensure that the national interest is not seriously jeopardised in the give-and-take of negotiation. To this aspect of our problem, the extent to which 'progressive' social policies within a state tend towards the elimination of the sources of war, we must return in a later chapter.

There is a third place in which men have sought the reason why nations sometimes become involved in war, in spite of the tragic absurdity of imagining that anything can be usefully gained by such destruction. This is in the anarchy of international relations in the strict sense—the absence of formal structures and institutions of law and government to bring the relations of states with each other into a coherent, manageable and tolerable order. Just as civil societies have sought protection from the dominance of the strong, and the unstable passions of the crowd, in complex systems of law and government, so it is contended that we cannot hope for an end to the constant threat of war until we have developed practical means on an international plane for providing individual states with two fundamental requirements—the assurance that their existence as states will not be threatened by their neighbours, and the means whereby conflicts of interest can be composed in terms of some sort of justice rather than of raw power. Security for a nation's life itself, and the sense that contentions will be resolved fairly between states—these are the only terms on which nations could be induced to forego the possibility of defending themselves by, if necessary, attacking their neighbours. According to this analysis, the reason why nations make war on each other is simply that no machinery exists to prevent them. Peace is inaccessible unilaterally. It requires not only that individual states pursue non-aggressive policies, but that they be provided with an environment of other states in which it is no longer reasonable to apprehend attack. War is not simply the expression of the acquisitiveness of a nation and the defensive reaction of its

victim. It is also, and far more often, the product of uncertainty
about what others will do, or the attempt to anticipate possible
policies of profitable aggression. Rousseau put the matter thus:

> It is quite true that it would be much better for all men to
> remain always at peace. But so long as there is no security for this,
> everyone, having no guarantee that he can avoid war, is anxious
> to begin it at the moment which suits his own interest and so
> forestall a neighbour, who would not fail to forestall the attack in
> his turn at any moment favourable to himself, so that many wars,
> even offensive wars, are rather in the nature of unjust precautions
> for the protection of the assailant's own possessions than a device
> for seizing those of others. However salutary it may be in theory
> to obey the dictates of public spirit, it is certain that, politically and
> even morally, those dictates are liable to prove fatal to the man
> who persists in observing them with all the world when no one
> thinks of observing them towards him.[4]

Here is the echo of the perpetual assertion of statesmen that it
is not they who are warlike, but others, and that the energy they
feel bound to exert in deterring or forestalling attack is no more
than the basic requirement which self-protection dictates. It is by
no means always sheer hypocrisy that lies behind such assertions,
but rather the awareness that security for a state must be at the
mercy of any and every possible opponent unless either it can
defend itself or else form some sort of alliance of those with
similar interests within which it can find protection.

Those who see our contemporary predicament in this light are
therefore led to argue that in the nuclear age we have no alternative but to create some form of world government—except,
sooner or later, a holocaust. Before, however, jumping as far as
that conclusion, we should glance at the lesser devices men have
invented to handle the problem. No doubt, historically, peace
has often been most secure over large areas of the world when
there existed some sort of imperial authority imposing its
own conviction of order, upon the smaller nations. China on one
side of the world and Rome on the other may have given many
cause to complain of the refusal to them of 'self-determination,'
but in the confusion which followed the barbarian attack on
each there were also many voices raised to lament the passing of

---

[4] J.-J. Rousseau, *A Lasting Peace*, tr. Vaughan, p. 123.

some sort of structure of order and administration. So also during the briefer period of the modern imperialism of Britain and, to a lesser degree, France. While it is now popular to recall only the repressive and negative aspects of that experience, a truer perspective will also recall the forceful suppression of inter-tribal warfare and the benefits accruing to innumerable humble individuals through the control of lesser oppressive powers by a greater one.

But however we call the score on the imperial solution, there is no conceivable possibility that men will settle for it in the long run. The price thus to be paid for peace is not one which will be indefinitely accepted. The 'protection money' includes an accept-ance of second-class citizenship for all but the ruling group; and while this may be tolerable for a time if the only alternative is the worse condition of total anarchy, it cannot remain so. Just as peaceful conditions begin to blot from memory the ugly features of an earlier dark age, so the human spirit begins once again to revolt against subjection and to cry again for freedom. And while the imperial solution was always in principle a passing phase, in modern conditions it is unthinkable. It is not only that human self-consciousness has advanced to the point where it will not tolerate subjection to other human wills as a permanent status. In a period where production is dominated by science and technology the human capacity for understanding and re-sponsible decision has perforce to be so far developed from childhood upwards that men are educated for ever out of the willingness to accept a measure of servitude.

The other means to which men have turned to secure some degree of stability and some tolerable conditions of international relations in a world where states retained their sovereign in-dependence, and so countenanced the basic conditions for inter-national anarchy, has been the balance of power. This reaction to the problem has always had a bad press in the United States of America, and for this and other reasons it has suffered a kind of caricature. It has not been sufficiently noted that the object of seeking and sustaining a balance of power is, in so far as it is consciously pursued, a deliberate attempt to prevent the emer-gence of new imperialisms. In this way of handling international relations, wars are prevented by ensuring that there are at least

two major alliances in rough equilibrium, neither of which is
sufficiently preponderant to threaten the other. Moreover, both
have a common interest in ensuring that no one else disturbs the
balance they have laboured to maintain. Within such a balance a
larger area of freedom is available to many groups and communities than is possible under imperialism. The trouble is its
instability; its proneness to collapse into disaster over what
appears superficially to be a very minor matter. Thus A. A.
Milne described the first World War as one in which ten million
men died because Austria-Hungary sought, unsuccessfully, to
avenge the death of one archduke. But as Winston Churchill has
pointed out: 'Small matters are only the symptoms of the
dangerous disease, and are only important for that reason. De-
hind them lie the Interests, the passions and the destiny of
mighty races of men; and long antagonisms express themselves
in trifles.'[5] Cobden may have been right in detail in saying in
1849 'that it is almost impossible, on looking back for the last
hundred years, to tell precisely what any war was about'. But a
major factor is always likely to have been the sensitivity, within a
European continent of tightly packed sovereign states, to the
dangerous potentialities of any jolt to the precarious balance of
power—giving warning that some new overmastering constellation of power was beginning to emerge.

Evidently today we survive in large part because some balance
exists between the major powers. So we do well not to deride this
solution too hastily. In so far as we depend on such a balance to
preserve some vestige of international order, we need to be ready
to pay the price. Thus there may well be occasions when the
preservation of the balance of power becomes an over-riding
objective of policy, and when it would be irresponsible and
wrong for a nation to prefer a line of action which appealed more
directly to its sense of the morally good. To bring down the frail
house of our world order so as to indulge a view of the abstract
good is scarcely to be commended. This consideration has not
always been appreciated by some of those committed to uni-
lateral nuclear disarmament in Britain. Furthermore, there are
many other kinds of discipline and frustration involved in keep-

[5] Winston S. Churchill, *The World Crisis*, vol. i, p. 52.

ing going so delicate a piece of machinery. These have to be consciously accepted. In reading descriptions of the public mood in the Britain of 1914 one is impressed by the sense of relief with which men laid aside the irritations and perplexities of a policy aimed at juggling with a balance of power, and welcomed the comparatively simpler solution of submitting their affairs to the crude arbitrament of force. A. A. Milne would have been more accurate if he had asserted that ten million men died because their leaders had exhausted their capacity to keep a balance trimmed. That is at least a warning to us in the nuclear age.

It is a dissatisfaction with such solutions, and a search for some system of international control, voluntarily accepted but capable of effective enforcement, which lies behind such twentieth century institutions as the League of Nations and the United Nations. But of course they have a much older history, running back in Europe to all the attempts of serious men to find a way of security and peace out of the disorder of the Dark Ages, following the disintegration of the *Pax Romana*. After the Reformation, such enterprises were often closely interwoven with ecumenical interests, reflecting the conviction that any accepted system of international authority must be rooted in a genuine unity of aspiration about the fundamental nature and destiny of human life. So Leibnitz could summarize his dreams thus: '... when union (in Europe) will be achieved, catholicity will be restored, Germany and the Latin world will recover their spiritual communion, the United Province and England will in their turn re-enter a Church at once Roman and reformed, and believers, all believers, will oppose the forces of disintegration that threaten their faith.'[6] There is, incidentally, something curiously up-to-date about these words, written in 1691.

Much of the thinking about this method of achieving peace started from the dictum of Pierre Dubois, a pioneer in this subject, who wrote in the early fourteenth century: 'To ensure peace, it is not enough to praise its benefits or even to agree to keep it. War must be prevented by suitable institutions'. This anticipates the later way of putting the same thing, that wars occur because there is nothing to prevent them doing so. Dubois

[6] Leibnitz, letter to Mme Brinon, Sept. 29, 1691, quoted in Voyenne, *Petite histoire de l'idée européene* (2nd ed., 1954), p. 90.

thought in terms of a European confederation (giving his project the unpeaceful title *Of the Recovery of the Holy Land*). Many centuries later Europeans took the hint in North America and created a union of states complete with institutions designed to prevent interstate conflicts from reaching military proportions. History was to prove that such institutions could not be finally effective till they had been challenged in a bloody civil war, and established on the basis of military victory. But it was also to prove how men could contrive to augment, each decade, the central power without surrendering too much human freedom. Before that, in Europe, the seventeenth century heard men like Sully and William Penn urge 'suitable institutions' to keep the peace in that contentious continent—for example, a General Assembly at which all sovereigns would have permanent ambassadors, also a common European army, a European Diet, Parliament or State.

The conflicting claims of self-determination and international order; the urgent necessity to create institutions capable of forestalling nuclear war; the fear of submitting our fate to men whom we suspect may be nourished by a different idea of the good life from our own (indeed, whose idea of the good life may include our elimination or slavery)—this is the contemporary expression of an old dilemma. Those who have attempted to resolve it by struggling to create and maintain a balance of power have, in Europe, shared a very considerable religious and cultural heritage. And a feature of their solution has been that it has left space for men to grow and breathe (for example the young nations) in a world where the great powers effectively stalemate each other. Similiarly, those in the United States of America who looked for an answer to the problem in terms of a central authority, hedged about by a written constitution and a sophisticated apparatus of divided powers so that it could not become unduly oppressive of human freedom, also sprang from a common stock—to the extent that the dominance of the old New England establishment only now gives way before other, more various social forces, and only after the old original culture has firmly set the pattern of America's political structure. The question is whether, on a universal scale, we are even distantly in sight of that necessary degree of basic agreement (represented visibly by religious institutions and practices, and invisibly by a whole host of unwritten assumptions and systems of approval and disapproval which form a culture) on which common institutions can be built. This is the subject to be further explored in Chapter VII. It can also be regarded from the other point of view—what sort of international institutions are conceivable and workable in a world of nations and cultures representing wide divergencies of conviction? After all, the modern state no longer bases its unity formally on some kind of religious or cultural uniformity. How does it manage to harmonise or tolerate wide varieties of opinion? We shall find ourselves struggling with some of the ultimate questions raised by the concept of the secular state, and seeking ways of projecting lessons learnt in that microcosmic context on to the world scene. We shall also have to ask the question whether religions, ideologies, and basic convictions are merely (as Marx maintained) devices we invent for ourselves to justify actions which would otherwise trouble our consciences—rationalisations of a kind later explored by modern psychology—or whether the illusion lies in imagining we either can or do manage to conduct our lives without anything of the sort.

At each of the three points at which we have approached the subject of seeking a remedy for our warlike proclivities, we have run into a problem which deserves separate treatment. It is the issue just referred to in the last paragraph. Does our hope for peace lie in the gradual evaporation of those divisive dogmatisms which we espouse from time to time in order to give heightened significance to our human lives? The question arises in each of the three contexts. If the root cause of war is that men's minds are in servitude to illusions of every kind from which it is possible to free them (inherited but anachronistic cultural patterns, misunderstandings about each other, blindness to our common interests and humanity), is there simply available as an alternative a more rational attitude to one another which would assure us all that we have no serious disagreements? Have we no serious disagreements once our personal security and bodily needs are assured? Is what men have grandly called 'the nobler aspirations of the human spirit' an optional extra, which in the world of automation might properly become 'leisure time activity'? This would imply that the rest of our common life, the serious business as it were, could somehow be controlled without raising any fundamental issues. But the likelihood is rather that it would be controlled by some very definite assumptions about what the good life was, all the more inflexible and subject to unquestioning conformity in so far as men wished to pretend to themselves that no such assumptions existed, and that all they insisted upon was 'a bit of common sense'.

The same question raised its head when we considered whether the internal structure of states harboured the real seeds of war, and whether in some sort of liberal or democratic or socialistic national pattern there lay a guarantee that a nation would never take up arms against its neighbours. We glimpsed some of the inhibitions to bellicosity which derived from a state structure responsive to the common will. But we saw too that it is precisely this kind of state which rouses itself to war only when it has been brought to believe that the issue at stake is not cynical or purely self-regarding but in some way is of transcendental dimensions. Conflict on that basis, as men have found in all wars of religion, tends to be savage in conduct and obstinate in rejecting resolution by means other than total victory.

Thirdly, we referred to the shrunken size of the world and the nature of modern weapons, and saw that this gave new force to the contention that we must now have effective international institutions to assure national security and resolve international dispute. At the same time, we added that these modern developments do not necessarily supply any new resources of common conviction on which such institutions could be based. Once again we have to face frankly that while men will fight for their own immediate material advantage, if there is reasonable prospect that their advantage will be promoted by doing so, they are liable to be much less rational and much more irreconcilable when they are persuaded that something more than their advantage is at issue. They might well be persuaded to accept the disciplines of international authority to resolve and suppress the first type of conflict, but only if they were assured that such authority did not become the instrument of men opposed to

B   33

them at a deeper level. Once again we run into a consideration of the part played in creating wars by those profound, unarguable myths, prejudices, ideologies or rationalisations which we all use to give shape and depth to our human existence.

One has to beware of a false profundity at this point. Obviously there are multitudes of human quarrels which originate, and even occasionally terminate, over quite simple issues that cannot by any stretch of the imagination be inflated into matters of ultimate concern. Francis I, when asked what profound differences accounted for the constant wars between him and his brother-in-law Charles V, is reputed to have answered: 'None whatever. We agree perfectly. We both want control of Italy!' But such issues are less likely today to be of themselves the fuse of war. 'War is expensive in its methods and unpredictable in its outcome; and these elements of expense and unpredictability have both grown enormously over the last hundred years,' writes Professor Michael Howard. He goes on: 'If war could be made to pay, as it did for the Dutch merchants in the seventeenth century and the English in the eighteenth, then its declaration was as welcome as its termination was deplored.' But by 1914 'the size and expense of the war-machines, and the uncertainty of the consequences of war for society as a whole, made violence an increasingly unusable instrument for the conduct of international affairs.... Indeed so great was the expense of modern war, so heavy were the sacrifices it entailed, that it was difficult to conceive of causes warranting it at all. Could the national resources really be mobilised and the youth of the nation really be sacrificed for anything short of national survival, or some great ideological crusade? So at least it appeared to the great Western democracies in the 1930s; and it was this sentiment that Hitler exploited with such superb and sinister skill.'[7] The sentiment is the stronger today when nuclear weapons make serious war even more unpredictable in its results, and open up unimaginable possibilities of disaster. But the corollary is that nowadays wars are associated with ideological confrontations of novel and terrible intensity.

[7] Professor Michael Howard, Inaugural Lecture in King's College, London, on the occasion of the foundation of a Chair of Military Studies in the University of London.

Men are heard frequently to ask themselves whether, in these circumstances, anything in heaven or earth is so important as the avoidance of war. The word coined to describe the policies which arise from such a state of mind is 'co-existence'. Is it not true that every nation, every ideology, has its element of guilt or deceit? Why make ultimate issues of matters upon which it may be possible to hold two opinions without logical contradiction? Just as the Europe of the seventeenth century, anaemic from the blood-letting of the wars of religion, made a primary virtue of tolerance and looked askance at aggressive dogmatisms, so the world of the later twentieth century, wounded and frightened by two world wars, hopes to escape a more awful war by trying to assure itself that nothing is worth fighting about.

But it will not work. The necessary twenty years of exhaustion have passed and a generation arises which does not know the agonies of mind and body suffered by those who embarked upon, and then endured, the Second World War. And we live in a world where men insist that human life has a significance which must not be gainsaid, however we struggle to define it. The issue of racial oppression simply cannot be made into a matter of secondary consequence, and it could easily become a cause of initiating war, unpredictable in its outcome. The coloured majority of mankind is driven to insist that the privileged few acknowledge that their lives have as much significance as anyone else's—and perhaps rather more than the white man's in so far as he is now recognised as being in a small minority on this planet. Again, modern man, rootless in the industrial cities, seeks to save his life from triviality and oblivion by finding a significant group to act as a projection of his own dignity. Nationalisms old and new lift up their heads, sometimes enlarged to continental proportions, and claim an ardent loyalty that seeks appropriate expression. Cultural, ethnic and linguistic cohesions claim and receive allegiance to provide men with a sense of their significance in time and space; and each of them proliferates a myth of its own importance. Such myths and assertions of value usually contain a strong element of glorification, an expression of the desire to affirm that human life is not merely nasty, brutish and short, which it sometimes appears to be. But often also there is a more precise claim for justice, freedom and the right to be one's original self. All such collections of loyalties and demands are directed in the first place at the heads of any who appear to deny them. They are a permanent refutation of the stability of co-existence as a satisfying way of life.

This universal human insistence on ascribing to man's life in history qualities which history itself can never fully confirm forces us to attend to the problem of meaning as an element in creating conditions for international peace. The question is sometimes asked why we do not all put away our arms and co-operate to exploit the material resources of the earth. One reason is that at heart many men do not believe that exploiting the material resources of the earth provides an adequate meaning for their lives. We are urged to eschew ambition (a quality which, when we wish to commend it, we call aspiration) and settle peaceably for the fullest relishing of the *status quo*. But many find the *status quo* intolerable, and all men of character object to the idealising of that form of human life most closely approximating to the regimen of contented dairy cattle. We are at odds with the vitalities, the imagination and the self-understanding of men when we try, in a false mood of rationalism, to belittle their dreams.

The problem, however, will show itself on examination to consist of two complementary parts. How do we take account of men's desire and insistence that life should not be understood in trivial terms? And how do we cope with the human tendency to give ultimate significance to that which is relative and temporary? This will form the subject of the enquiry in Chapter VIII. It will raise perhaps in the most explicit form that which is implicit in much else in this book—the role which religious conviction plays in making life on earth both more intractable and more hopeful, and in particular the contribution which the Christian faith ought to make to world peace.

2

THE DANGERS OF MORALISING

IN THE SEARCH for reversible causes of war in the previous chapter, we began with the view of those who seek in the minds of men the real sources of bellicosity in the sense that the cultures they accept and live with involve behaviour patterns and value judgements which tend to this end inevitably; or that irrational war-making is an expression of psychological inadequacies, looking for satisfaction in this direction; or that in a very particular way unfamiliarity with each other, worked upon by fear and suspicion, leads to aggressive-defensive reactions. The cures proposed respectively would therefore be: the conscious reform of our cultural patterns; the establishment of some means of identifying psychological faults in those aspiring to positions of power, so that they could be cured or prevented from achieving responsibility beyond their capacity; and the promotion of every conceivable programme for enabling people to get to know one another as they actually are. The limitations of each of these nostrums were seen to be significant. The second and third prescriptions especially reflect a curious unfamiliarity with the nature of the human species. On the one hand, the drives and urges which send a man in search of power and public responsibility are more closely linked with his tendency to dominate and even destroy than is here recognised. On the other hand, familiarity is an experience based on trust (the factor in short supply in any case), and familiarity does not necessarily mean approval or even acceptance in the end.

It is the first aspect of this type of approach which can provide at least a starting point for serious reflection on our duty as citizens and human beings to create the conditions of peace in our world. Allowing it to be somewhat grandiose to describe our task as the creation of a new kind of culture; and granting that the time-scale involved in such a project, anyway, is far too leisurely for the emergency situations of the modern nuclear age—nevertheless we cannot escape the conviction that in some way the personal attitudes of people are important in creating conditions of peace. It is this conviction which we shall explore further in this chapter.

This is the field in which it is commonly assumed that religion, and particularly the Christian religion, presumes to specialise. It is believed to make its contribution in one of two ways—either by the production of human characters which are specially 'good' (at least in the sense that they will be prepared to absorb a lot of hostility and exploitation without starting trouble), or by laying down and declaring rules and regulations concerning moral behaviour, which will have the effect of denouncing, not preventing, man's inhumanity to man. The second is the more familiar, and the one most generally understood to represent typical religious activity. Many thinking people, who themselves find no strong attraction in the dogma and ceremonies of classical Christianity, nevertheless expect and value from the churches a certain clarity and definition of moral judgement. This is particularly so in the sphere of international relations and nuclear war. The very enormity of the disaster confronting the human race, if it fails to resolve the problem of war, prompts all sensible people to recruit every possible resource of mind and spirit to avert the horror. However anachronistic intellectually the churches may appear, they may still in practice have a useful role in supplying a moral bulwark against the descent into unlimited savagery. This service the churches have been ready obligingly to supply, a little glad perhaps for even so small a sign that the community is ready to accord them this limited relevance. The question to be investigated is, whether and in what sense such activity is valid. In this chapter the question will be asked in terms of the situation itself, without theological presuppositions. In the next, it will be considered in relation to the Christian faith with a view to determining how far the popular assumption of the relevance of that faith in this particular way is true.

First, we need to distinguish two familiar ways of conceiving the nature of moral judgement, and then to outline a third possibility. Men whose experience of life has taught them the strength of their own passions and the ungovernable element in their own wills tend to picture the function of the moral law as being somewhat alien to their wayward natures—coming as a schoolmaster to correct and check their wilder impulses, to set limits to what is permissible. For them, morals are conceived in legal terms and the good life in terms of obedience. They have to discipline the many and competing urges of their own natures into some sort of coherence, and to do this they rely on their sense of obligation to a law which is beyond the reach of their own whims and fancies. Moreover, they conceive of good behaviour in public life as that which does not transgress moral rules. This is perhaps the most immediately recognisable type of religious approach to public questions, and to the problems of war and peace in particular, having many distinguished spokesmen at the present time whose moral protests are of a kind which attract widespread publicity. Thinking of this kind puts absolutely first the query 'what is right?' rather than the question 'what do you achieve by sticking to your principles?' To the objection that the course of action proposed ought to show some reasonable hope of ameliorating the human situation in one way or another, two possible responses are relied on. One is that if you do what is right the results are automatically and inevitably better, even if you cannot yourself foresee all the consequences. The other is that the moral obligation is ultimate and the consequences must be left to look after themselves.

Before looking more closely at this way of thinking, the other familiar approach must be considered. This is characteristic of the man whose nature is more absorbed by the world around him than by the civil war within himself. The disorder which attracts his attention is that of his environment, and his ambition is the creation of new expressions of his own vision of what is good or pleasant or attractive in the world he lives in. The justification he seeks for his actions is that they are rightly directed to attain a good end. The 'object of the exercise' is the criterion by which men's behaviour is to be judged—is the end sought truly desirable, noble, and to the general advantage?

The typical commendation in this category is that a man worked for a noble ideal, rather than in conformity to a strict rule.

The intense heat which can be generated between people holding these different positions, when they are confronted by choices of policies, not least in the sphere of international behaviour, is a matter of common knowledge. A number of familiar clichés will certainly be employed and the argument can become acrimonious as to whether the means are justified by the end, whether one must submit to compromises of principle for the sake of making any impression upon events, and whether we have grasped the revolutionary consequences of all kinds which would flow from the readiness of a number of people to do what they believed right, come what may. The fact is, of course, that the attempt by either party to claim that its analysis is completely satisfactory in itself is misleading. An action cannot be judged out of all relation to the consequences that will most likely flow from it. We cannot afford, therefore, to leave out of account the calculation of the ends which an action will serve. On the other hand, there are certain kinds of action which we instinctively sense to be impossible to justify even by the most sophisticated demonstration that they would further a worthy cause. The perception that in some way both considerations are required for balanced judgement should push us on to seek a more inclusive and satisfying criterion. Before attempting this, however, we must look in greater detail at some of the very practical difficulties which arise when either of these familiar forms of moral criticism are brought to bear in the realm of international politics.

When moral judgement is conceived in terms of law and principle, we are faced with two different kinds of frustration in our attempt to bring such judgement to bear on the issues arising in our daily newspaper. One derives from the fact that, when we are rigidly honest with ourselves, we observe that it is possible to describe the moral issue in more than one way. There is, as a rule, more than one moral issue involved. An international conflict can be described in terms of the right of a people to self-determination, to have a controlling say in their own destiny. Those who then oppose a solution along the appropriate lines will often find it possible to moralise their objections in terms of the duty of a nation to avoid actions which threaten to lead to international incidents. This is one example of the eternal dilemma of reconciling freedom and order, both being good things. Another way of putting the same thing is by considering the relation between peace and justice. How much injustice is it tolerable to connive at, rather than risk the outbreak of violence on an international scale? Or when is a war of liberation justified? The general tendency of contemporary moralists is to emphasise the over-riding evil of war itself, particularly in view of the possibility of its escalation, so that if violence breaks out other aspects of the problems are put aside in favour of general appeals to cease fire. Is this a correctly balanced moral judgement, or is it the choice of one of several moral issues involved, a choice determined chiefly by apprehension of the immediate consequences? If it is the latter, then we are in the position where moral judgement is derived, not from some clear principle but from a calculation (or miscalculation) of consequences. In that case, we are vulnerable to criticism as to the accuracy of our forecast of events, and must justify our protest by showing that we have been as assiduous in the careful calculation of consequence as those whom we criticise. At least we cannot fall back on the moralist's home ground, and maintain that one simple moral issue is at stake. In practice, we find that a serious attempt to reach a sound moral appreciation of the great issues between the nations always involves us in an attempt to balance competing considerations, so that we have no process of slide-rule certainty for reaching a decision.

The other element of frustration in trying to bring to bear on international conflicts a clear moral judgement arises from the fact that the moral aspects are inextricably interwoven with the technical. The tendency of those who think in terms of moral law is to imagine moral principles as creating a kind of ring-fence through which men must not try to break out. A very familiar example of this kind of thought is to be found in the doctrine of the just war. This is a body of wisdom full of practical usefulness in directing our minds to rational and sober and humane considerations regarding the conduct of war. But of its nature this doctrine does not so much prescribe a course of action as draw attention to the limits which any action should observe. It is in this sense that we may describe it as representing the 'ring-fence' type of morality. At its crudest, this system of morality tends to render permissible all action within the given limits, and to condemn all outside. Thus it can be applied to the relation of the sexes in such a way as to render indifferently acceptable many kinds of action within the bonds of matrimony, and equally indifferently unacceptable all physical relations outside that bond. It is therefore not so much a way of life as a kind of rather arbitrary boundary line, somewhat exterior to the main business of living; a resented obstruction rather than a road to fulness of life. But if, in reaction, men seek direction for their lives in a form more integrally related to the factors they know they must consider already, then that moral direction will be found to be unbreakably associated with judgements of a technical, amoral nature. Should Britain, for instance, continue to exercise an influence east of Suez? The question raises a host of issues, one of which is whether in so doing she would be rendering a service, perhaps, to India or Malaysia, in the discharge of which she would put herself in such a financial position that she was compelled to cease other urgent services to India. The answer to that is not to be found in moral considerations, but in highly technical economic calculations associated with other judgements about the cheapest way of fulfilling certain military commitments. Yet these very calculations are highly relevant to a moral concern as to what is the right thing for Britain to do. The upshot of these considerations is that there is no prospect that perplexities will be simplified, and awkward dilemmas resolved, if only we see our problems as moral ones. The reverse is rather the case—that the contradictions and competing claims already present to our minds in assessing the sheer practicalities of action in the circumstances before us, are now augmented by moral contradictions and competing claims. Instead of simplifying the issue, the effect is to add a further dimension of choice. This is no reason for pushing moral considerations aside, though it is probably in practice one of the chief factors which tempts busy men to do so. They more often show repugnance towards considering moral aspects of political questions because they shrink from entering upon a daunting and perplexing effort than because they desire to pursue immoral ends. In turn, those who champion moral causes tend to dodge the difficulty to which we have referred by greatly oversimplifying the issues.

All of this argument is worth pursuing carefully if thereby some light is thrown on a controversy which traditionally bedevils the co-operation of 'men of goodwill', and in particular Christian churchmen, in the field of international politics. It can be crudely described as the argument between the pacifists and the non-pacifists, though this definition would require elaborate refining before it became really adequate. For one thing, each of the two categories thus referred to covers a great variety of opinion; and for another, adherence to, or rejection of, the pacifist position is only one symptom of a style of approach which has many other visible consequences. But for immediate purposes, simply to indicate a connexion rather than exhaust a subject, we may use these broad categories to make a point. Those who think of the moral aspects of international questions in terms of upholding certain permanently valid principles, of doing the right thing come what may—restoring moral earnestness to the cynical game of politics by adopting the position of 'Here I stand; I cannot budge whatever the consequences'—are bound to find themselves at odds with those whose cast of mind is at once more idealistic and pragmatic. The latter will often be prepared to concede a point to gain a more important one, in the pursuit of a goal of great human value. Tactics will be flexible, and can take fully into account the less than noble inducements which urge men to act in a certain way, so long as sight is never lost of the end to be attained, and so long as the price to be paid *en route* never reaches the level where it can effectively halt the advance itself. It is not possible to say *ab initio* that either of these approaches is superior in moral integrity to the other. Equally it is idle to debate furiously specific practical policies between two sides, each starting from quite different moral premises. Evidently the debate is and will remain entirely futile until people are prepared to uncover and examine their two different ways of arriving at a moral judgement, and acknowledge the specific deviations which belong to each. If those who judge their actions in terms of the end to which they are directed are always in danger of losing sight of the objective in the fascination of tactical manoeuvres, then those who seek moral safety by sticking firmly to their principles run a risk of equal proportions—of being frivolous in the assessment of likely effects and of pretending that such moral judgements can cut through the tangle of our perplexities to a simplification which in fact is quite illusory. An even greater gain of such self-knowledge would be the joint pursuit of some more adequate and inclusive formulation of a pre-occupation both sides share —that international political decisions should be rescued from bondage to short-sighted expediency. Before attempting a modest contribution in this direction, there is, however, one more feature which in different degrees belongs in common to both these schools of moralists.

Whichever approach a man makes to the moral assessment of political choice, he is in any case liable, once he begins to take moral aspects at all seriously, to be drawn into the assessment, not only of his own actions but of other men's, of the actual conflicts in the world with which he is confronted, in terms of who is right and who is wrong. At least he will feel obliged to strike a balance of vice and virtue and to award marks. The curious fact is that in so doing he will not be bringing anything particularly novel into the argument, for the modern world is strident with the cries of men and nations lauding the moral seriousness of their causes. It is an illusion of many people of liberal or religious disposition that their fellows will neglect moral factors unless they are reminded. This illusion is often due, not so much to the seriousness with which such folk take morality, as to the seriousness with which they take themselves. Indeed there is a very strong case to be made for the contention that a situation which is already somewhat intractable between two parties to an international quarrel becomes utterly insoluble once it is moralised, and that this is the state of affairs in some of the most acute contemporary confrontations either of ideology or of race. As soon as either side becomes convinced that its cause is the cause of righteousness, the only outcome which is tolerable is the unconditional surrender of the opponent.

Thus at one blow is removed all possibility of finding the accommodations and compromises whereby conflicts are eased, without war and the doubtful fruits of victory. It becomes, in a curious way, the task of the man of moral earnestness to deflate the moral pretensions of nations as a contribution to peace. In so doing, he can avoid becoming insufferable only if he accepts a measure of such deflation as applying also to himself.

An example of this paradoxical situation is supplied by recent movements of opinion regarding war. For nearly twenty years after the end of the last Great War men's minds were properly obsessed by the dangers of another outbreak, this time with nuclear weapons in full use. The point was made all over the world that whatever might have been true in other ages, in the nuclear age war had become a complete anachronism. The moral judgement was urged that, in the event of conflict, certainly nothing would justify a demand for unconditional surrender, itself one of the great moral failures of the conduct by the Allies of World War II. The attempt to assert that 'conventional' war at least could still make some sense was regarded in many quarters with suspicion in so far as some recalled the 'conventional' destruction of Europe in the 1940s and the agony of its cities and peoples, and all knew the dangers of escalation. Yet many of those who were most seriously in earnest about these matters are now beginning to consider whether the moral case against the present Government of South Africa does not justify military initiatives precisely of the kind which previously seemed outlawed, even if in this case done under different auspices. The point of this reflection is not to open up for consideration one of the most passionately argued issues of our day, but simply to indicate the way in which a serious attempt to accord moral marks to the conflicts of peoples and nations always and inevitably tends towards a search for ways of making the delinquent side surrender. The more the moral judgement becomes absolute, the more the surrender required becomes unconditional, and the less likelihood exists of bringing it about with means other than war. There is a sense in which morals and peace are an ill-assorted couple, while adjustment, give-and-take, negotiation and compromise offer chances of abating conflict only at the risk of being termed unprincipled.

Professor Herbert Butterfield is one who has always seen clearly the dangerous possibilities associated with the obverse side of the coin of moral judgement in the sphere of international relations —the way in which men of limited self-knowledge can use an apparent moral earnestness to blind themselves to the realities of the situation. He writes:

'The more human beings are lacking in imagination, the more incapable men are of any profound kind of self-analysis, the more we shall find that their self-righteousness hardens, so that it is just the thick-skinned who are more sure of being right than anybody else. And though conflict might still be inevitable in history even if this particular evil did not exist, there can be no doubt that its presence multiplies the deadlocks and gravely deepens all the tragedies of all the centuries. At its worst it brings us to that mythical messianism—that messianic hoax—of the twentieth century which comes perilously near to the thesis: "Just one little war more against the last remaining enemies of righteousness, and then the world will be cleansed, and we can start building Paradise." '[1]

It may be added that there is no surer way of courting hostility than to call in question the conviction of a group that its cause is the cause of righteousness—better they feel, to take up arms and fight it out than set the serpent of doubt roaming amongst their moral certainties! For men gropingly discern that unless there is some objective basis for reaching a judgement of right and wrong, life has lost significance and the abyss of meaninglessness opens at their feet. This terrible possibility gives desperation to their arms.

These truisms provoke us to seek a more refined and discriminating definition of what it is we are, and ought to be, truly concerned for in our blundering attempts to find guide lines for our international choices more universal, objective and significant than the expediency of the moment. Richard Niebuhr offers a useful clue in the Robertson Lectures delivered in Glasgow in 1960 and posthumously published under the title *The*

[1] Herbert Butterfield, *Christianity and History* (London: Bell, 1949), p. 41.

46

Responsible Self[2] After outlining the two foregoing ways of going about moral discrimination, associated with the two images we may have of ourselves as man-the-maker whose actions are determined by the purposes he espouses, and man-the-citizen, living under law, Dr Niebuhr develops a third and more dynamic approach associated with the word 'responsibility'. In this case man is conceived of as the 'answerer', responding more or less appropriately to action upon him—man engaged not in some private moral soliloquy but in a sort of dialogue with his environment. From this point of view, right action depends on his interpreting correctly what is in fact happening to him and making the appropriate rejoinder. There is a recognition of the fact that human beings are part of a general historical process in which their own decisions and choices mesh. So in order to answer the question 'What shall I do?' a man would not first consider 'What is my goal, ideal or purpose?', nor again 'What is the law and what is the first law of my life?' The real prior question to be answered would rather be 'What is going on? What is happening?' If the first type seeks the good, and the second the right, then the third looks for the fitting—the action that fits into the situation of interaction as it really is and anticipates in turn a fitting response. Such a position involves not only that we record accurately the events going on around us, but that we understand aright their meaning. Once again we note the intrusion of this obstinate term into our discussion. The point can be neatly put by saying that our moral imperatives derive from a proper grasp of our indicatives and a true understanding of their basic significance. We anticipate later chapters if we say that the question to be considered is not whether we *ought* to be responsible, nor whether responsibility is a worthy goal, but 'To whom or what are we responsible, and in what community of interaction do I in fact find myself?' In his use of the word 'responsible', Dr Niebuhr gives it a many-coloured meaning. It includes a recognition of the simple fact that the situation in which I have to make a choice is not of my initiating, but comes

---

[2] New York and London: Harper and Row, 1963. Of course the use of the concept of 'responsibility' in ethical judgement is not original to Richard Niebuhr. I have chosen his formulations for their clarity. But a more profound, if more involved, discussion is to be found in Dietrich Bonhoeffer's *Ethics*, specially in Chapter VI.

at me with a challenge or demand of its own. I am responding. But my response is not mere reflex action. It is also an act of recognition of the significance of what is occurring, and is responsible therefore in a deeper sense. Moreover, it is not an act which ends the matter, but one rather which continues a whole process so that I must expect to have to answer again for that which flows from my choice, and in this sense too I am answerable and responsible.

'Freedom is the recognition of necessity' say the Marxists and point in a direction not far away from the one to which we are looking. For them right action is determined by a scientific appreciation of the forces in society and how they operate. Much of the political effectiveness of communist groups in certain situations has derived in the past from the intellectual rigour of their analysis of the situation, so that they really understood far better than their opponents what was going on, and could act more 'responsibly'. Most of the failures of Marxists have arisen from the fact that a rigid doctrine and ideology has blinded them either to the full nature of what was happening around them or to the true significance of events—and has nourished a fairy tale credulity which believed reports because the doctrine had prophesied such developments, or a view of man and the universe which seriously misunderstood their real significance. What is required of us is to seek to give a more accurate account of the nature of the historical events in which we are involved, and a more complete recognition of that to which, or to whom, we are responding and responsible.

Such a procedure throws us back into the world of indicatives as prior to that of imperatives. It goes contrary to that element in contemporary humanist thinking which hopes to remain sceptical in the realm of what it would term 'dogma', and at the same time retain its right to be extremely positive and assured in the realm it would call ethical. The passion with which men of this persuasion espouse the cause of human justice and exhibit genuine devotion in the service of needy fellows is to be regarded with the most humble respect, even when it seems to exhibit a certain contempt for any who see the situation any way differently. But ultimately all such natural compassion is in mortal danger of disillusion and despair unless, as the Marxists so clearly see, it can be made to seem fitting in terms of the reality with which we have to deal.

We have here a possible way of stating what two types in our contemporary society are affirming in their rejection of traditional moral formulations. There are the growing number of scientifically trained minds whose solution for a problem tends to be sought in technical terms. They feel a certain impatience with people who state their case in terms of great ideals, or of moral precepts, for they sense that this has the effect of bringing passion to play where cool heads and perceptive calculations can be more rewarding. An illustration in our field can be found among those who have provided the driving force in the creation of the European Economic Community. Many of them could have made their case mainly in terms of the visionary aim of rendering inter-European war for ever impossible by abolishing national frontiers. This indeed was in their minds. They could also have presented it as a great moral gesture of reconciliation, which it certainly was. These ideas provided, as it were, the latent dream. But what filled the day's work was a realistic and highly expert assessment of the actual forces at work, and the search for technical means to manipulate these forces in such a way that they found their own fulfilment in serving a larger enterprise. These men have been called 'technocrats', not always by way of compliment; but they would not necessarily repudiate the appellation, nor allow that it implied an absense of serious moral purpose. Rather they could say that the success so far achieved has arisen from the accuracy of their technical appreciation of what was happening to Europe, coupled with an understanding of the nature and destiny of the human enterprise; and that their achievement is the marrying of practical techniques to the demands of the historical occasion—the discovery of what is *fitting* in view of all the circumstances. But the circumstances would, for many of them, be held to include much beyond the purely technical, economic or political, and indeed would be considered to embrace realities in the realm of dogma and the meaning of life.

The other type whom we recognise as being cool to traditional moral formulations are those serious-minded members of the younger generation who have discovered the inherent dishonesty of their elders in seeking to impose moral conformity which lacks intellectual justification. 'Who says so?' is a very proper rejoinder to those whose chief justification for imposing courses of behaviour on us appears to be a timid concern for social acceptance, or the avoidance of too costly an involvement in the life of our fellows. Nor is the question persuasively answered in the outmoded terms of Kant or the reiteration of religious assertions which have lost their conviction. It is, however, meaningful to discuss as best we can what our human nature is like, what are the conditions of real community life, and therefore what kind of action fits into the realities of the world of which we form a part. Even if such a discussion leads out into a landscape forbidding in its immensity and in the difficulty of discerning with any clarity what the main guiding features are, still it remains obligatory, imposed upon us if we are to avoid the frustration of a life spent banging our heads against a brick wall, just because we could not bear the risk of standing back and assessing life's limits and context with as much accuracy as we could manage.

It must now be asked whether an attempt to judge our actions in terms of this understanding of responsibility avoids the obstacles presented by the more traditional way of thinking. Morals as law presented us with two problems—the competition of conflicting laws which we face in any given historical situation, so that in the end we do not find ourselves firmly guided by a law but left with the responsibility of balancing claims inherently valid in themselves; and secondly, the inextricable confusion of technical and moral factors in any given decision, so that the moral aspect does not necessarily simplify and clarify decision but often adds just another range of perplexities. Now, without too exhaustive an examination, we can see at once that the formulation in terms of 'responsibility'—of responding fittingly to the challenge of the environment and occasion and being answerable thereafter in a continuous dialogue with the world of which we are a part—relieves some of these difficulties. Instead of importing into our picture of the problem in front of us a number of competing 'principles' which must then be juggled with at the cost of a lot of intellectual ingenuity so that they yield a kind of answer, we are now permitted to bury Plato, and to cease looking for eternal archetypes of behaviour. Instead we look at the question before us, seeking to find in the depth of the thing itself, properly understood, the right response. And further, we are no longer required to distinguish aspects termed 'technical' from those 'moral', but may consider the matter in its wholeness, realising that in one sense all questions are technical if that means an understanding of what is the appropriate way to respond to them. For many this will appear at first sight to be a highly dangerous debunking of all the signposts and recognised criteria on which civilised behaviour has relied, and an encouragement to adventures which can only lead to disaster. It is certainly an encouragement to adventure, and this is surely a merit at a time when so much of the familiar world in which the older rules were formed has passed away, and so much that is unprecedented becomes part of our daily experience. But it is an invitation to chaos only if we fail to articulate successfully some radical facts about the nature and meaning of our existence which will allow us to understand our environment and historical moment in depth. All depends on whether any intelligible and persuasive answer can be attempted in the realm of meaning rather than of 'morals'. This is the question which must be reserved for treatment at the end of all the other arguments of this book.

The other way of regarding moral judgement has traditionally been in relation to the end pursued. Here the classical difficulty has been to work out the relation of means and ends. The justification of many of the most horrific events of this century has been the conviction that they had to be accepted as the price to be paid for a new age for mankind. The connexion with the specific problem of war is obvious; and also with many other contemporary and key questions of governmental policy. How much hardship must be imposed on the present generation in a poor country in order to build up the investment which alone will offer better prospects to their grandchildren? That is one instance, and many more can be conceived. How far does a good end justify ruthless action to achieve it? The answer can, of course, be sought, and the problem apparently eased, by considering whether certain kinds of action, attractive for their immediate practicality, would not in fact inflict such wounds on the community in those invisible regions of mutual trust and co-operative enthusiasm, that they would not fulfill their apparent promise. But this is really to side-step an awkward question, for there may well be actions which would, on balance, benefit future generations more than damage them (so far as the human mind can judge), and from which, nevertheless, we shrink because we feel a duty to the present as well as the future. Evidently, the concept of the responsible action, at once answering to the immediacy of the real situation and also conceived as part of an on-going dialogue, provides us with a way of thinking which no longer tears apart the two aspects of the question. In it there is the hint that, if we understand aright the reality with which we have to deal in the present, action which is fitting in that respect will also be coherent as regards the future, in that we shall be working with the grain of events.

How far does this way of stating the case help us to avoid the bellicosities of self-righteousness? It may be that it simply shifts the initiative from the prigs to the opinionated, from those who protest their virtue to those who proclaim their ideology, from those who make moral judgements to those who rely on dogmatic assertions. This will have to be looked at more fully later. But for the moment let us at least allow that it may be marginally easier to handle a discussion about ideology and dogma, and to make profitable a controversy in such terms, than it is to reduce the confrontation of two groups persuaded of their virtue to talkable proportions. It is easier to have a debate between people who think each other mistaken or misled than between those convinced of each other's wickedness. A universe of discourse is presumed to exist in the one case which is specifically denied in the other; and the minimum of trust required to make dialogue possible is based not so much on acceptance of each other's theses as on the postulate of each other's good intentions. Moral estrangement is not a matter of argument, and as soon as it becomes so it is no longer moral estrangement.

The argument at this point therefore suggests that in so far as wars begin in the minds of men, the cure is not to be sought simply in the defence of moral principle. Indeed the world is everywhere strident with the noise of those who appeal to moral principle to justify their hostility to their enemies, the particular principle selected being that which best suits the complainant's interest or ministers to his sense of his own virtue. The place to start, it is suggested, in the search for that which will draw men together without requiring them to adopt a meaningless relativism in their estimation of themselves and their history, is a deeper understanding of the situation in which they are placed, a more realistic appreciation of that to which they are required to respond. Is this, rather than a changeless system of moral principles, the proper contribution of the Christian religion? This is the question to which the next chapter addresses itself.

3

THE REALISM OF THE BIBLE

So INGRAINED IS the habit of mind which assumes that the specific contribution of Christianity to the attainment of international peace lies in the field of moral judgement that it requires a considerable and conscious effort to put the matter in another light. We are agreed that if we are not to become playthings of the historical process, we need some criteria or standing-ground to give us the necessary distance from the process, so that we can make an independent judgement of the right course to follow. It is hoped however that we are also agreed that one of the great and liberating discoveries of the modern world is that every process we observe has its own inherent rules which we must recognise and respect if we are to respond intelligently to the challenge of events. From the moment Galileo attempted to make this point in relation to the observed facts of astronomy, there has been a running fight with theology, misunderstood as a science insisting on the acceptance of unquestionable assumptions before men had the right to report what they actually saw. The fight has been generally concluded, but in the realm of politics, and not least in international politics, the old habits linger tenaciously, insisting that at any rate in terms of morals the church has the ultimate right of censorship.

It has been the argument of the last chapter that a better approach is discoverable when we understand the contribution of Christianity otherwise. This contribution is made when Christianity, instead of insisting on eternal and unchangeable moral principle claiming an *a priori* authority, offers to give further illumination to our understanding of what we actually see going on in history. This contribution is then made in the indicative

54

rather than the imperative mood, or rather the imperatives are seen to arise naturally from our appreciation of the indicatives. The subject of the present chapter is to survey, however cursorily, the biblical tradition: to see what support it gives to this kind of approach; what in fact is the illumination it claims to offer of the human predicament; what is the nature of the independent criteria it proposes which will enable us better to find the way of peace in the world. The law as declared in the Old Testament, the Prophets, and finally the style and nature of the teaching of Jesus Christ must be looked at briefly in order to sketch some general conclusions.

Scholarship has made clear the dependence of the versions of what men call the Law of Moses on the teachings of the great prophets of the eighth century BC. Nevertheless, before attending to their own type of teaching, it is important to observe the nature of that which is called 'the Law' in ancient Jewish thought. For evidently we are dealing with a translation of a Hebrew word, and indeed with an English version of the Greek translation of the Hebrew so that there is ample opportunity for shades of meaning to fade away and new associations to come to the fore in this process of moving from one linguistic world to another. This is indeed precisely what has happened in this case. We must start with the Hebrew word *Torah*, which is what Moses declared, whatever it signified. The Greek version of the Old Testament current in the time of Jesus had already fixed *nomos* as the Greek equivalent of *torah* but the two words were not in origin equivalent. '*Torah* denotes the guidance or instruction which comes from God through the oracular utterances of the priests or through the prophets; it is the whole content of God's revelation of his nature and purpose, which incidentally makes clear man's responsibility before God. In so far as this responsibility is clarified by a collection of maxims into a legislative code, the term may be applied to such a code, and in this restricted sense it coincides with one meaning of *nomos*, a single enactment or the legal corpus of a given community....'[1] Whereas the Greek word conjured up something in the nature of

[1] W. A. Whitehouse, 'Law', in *A Theological Word Book of the Bible*, ed. A. Richardson (London: SCM Press, 1950).

a set of injunctions and commands requiring strict obedience, the Hebrew word went far beyond this. It encompassed 'the whole content of God's revelation of his nature and purpose', and in this respect can be properly regarded as the disclosure of the nature of the environment in which man's life is set. So it is declared as much in the indicative mood as in the imperative. Indeed the imperatives arise from the exhortation to act fittingly in such an environment. Seeing that Israel is called to life in relation to a God of the nature of Yahweh, there are certain kinds of action which are wholly inappropriate and out of character in such a situation, and other ways of behaving which are congruous with the facts of life. One type of activity works across the grain of the real situation and is therefore subject to constant frustration and futility; another is in accordance with the realities and 'goes with a swing'. So God is made to say to Moses, at the end of that great book of the Torah, Deuteronomy, 'See, I have set before thee this day life and good, and death and evil; in that I command thee this day to love the Lord thy God, to walk in his ways, and to keep his commandments and his statutes and his judgements, that thou mayest live and multiply, and that the Lord thy God may bless thee in the land whither thou goest in to possess it. But if thine heart turn away, and thou wilt not hear, but shall be drawn away, and worship other gods, and serve them (i.e. pursue fantasies); I denounce unto you this day that ye shall surely perish; ye shall not prolong your days upon the land, whither thou passest over Jordan to go in to possess it. I call heaven and earth to witness against you this day, that I have set before thee life and death, the blessing and the curse: therefore choose life, that thou mayest live, thou and thy seed' (Deuteronomy 30. 15-19). This is not merely a set of threats and promises associated with being bad or good, but a fair warning about the consequences of basing one's conduct on fairy tales conjured up by wishful thinking or nightmares evoked by despair. It is a true account of the advantages which flow from action which is in congruity with the real world we are living in—a world which is the playground neither of demons nor fairies but the field of action of an ultimate reality whose character was beginning to be discovered, but who remained hidden behind the mysterious name of Yahweh.

The contents of the Torah were thus twofold—on one hand, declarations of what Yahweh was like in character and what He was believed to be doing with His world; and then maxims about the types of behaviour fitting in that situation and therefore promising a more abundant and better life than any other way. It was not necessary to distinguish nicely between primitive food taboos which might very well have a basis in observed fact about hygiene in a hot climate; sabbatical injunctions which enshrined an understanding that to be human meant something more than to be part of the system of production (the getting and spending which necessarily preoccuppies most of our days); sexual regulations; the right way to treat strangers, the poor, neighbours and so on. All were in principle signposts to the way of life rather than the way of disease, perversion, conflict and destruction. And all stemmed from the fact that Yahweh was 'gracious', was on the side of human beings, and had specifically approached his people with a promise of full life, placing them under an obligation to respond by accepting this context as the whole frame and ground of the national life. Everything sprang from the kind of ultimate reality men found themselves dealing with.

Nor was this ultimate reality defined in general abstract categories. His nature and character appeared from the great deeds which God had done—from the first apparently small beginning with Abraham to the great climax under Moses when he swept Israel out of the hands of her oppressor across the Red Sea and into a limitless future. That sort of Yahweh was the only background there was for human life, so if you wanted to live and flourish you would do well to match your life to that. In this way the Torah did not appear as a burden but as something for which a Jew could never give enough thanks: a lamp to his feet, sweeter than honey, more to be desired than gold—curious words if one imagines one is considering what we normally think of as 'moral rules', which inevitably have a restrictive character and appear to block us from doing what we want. But intelligible if we can escape such false associations and realise that a man's heart is singing because he has found the right way to a full life.

It is extraordinarily difficult for us to bear constantly in mind that this was the nature of 'the law of the Lord' as understood in the Old Testament. Inevitably our minds turn back to a more familiar notion of law which is stern, limiting and forbidding. Nor is this our only difficulty. If we look in the Old Testament for moral rules of this sort we are horrified at what we find. For the kind of barbaric injunctions we discover, most especially in connexion with the conduct of war itself, appals the delicate sensitivities of many a modern humanist. A consideration of this matter is revealing. For whereas many a noble and sensitive person today makes do with some fearfully depersonalised concept of the nature of the ultimate reality in which our lives are set, he tends to make up for this by an insistence that our own behaviour be human—as if he were trying to defy the nature of our ambience and destiny. The Old Testament is far ahead of us in its perception that we live in a universe of which it is not misleading to expect a response of 'lovingkindness and tender mercy'. But the people of Israel were slow to discover the range and scope of that truly universal concern. They marvelled at the way Yahweh had treated them. They could not credit that so also he would treat the whole human race. If you go in search of moral rules in the Old Testament, you may well come back bewildered. If you seek there true descriptions of the environment in which we are called to live, you may be incredulous but scarcely disappointed. The Torah is, in Whitehouse's words, 'the whole content of God's revelation of his nature and purpose', and as such is seen to be precisely the declaration of the nature of the circumstances into which our lives have to fit if they are to make sense. The attempt to treat it legalistically, as rules to be rigorously applied, was the cause of some of Jesus Christ's sharpest reproofs.

Sabbath observance provides the clearest illustration. It is perfectly possible to conceive our days as an unending struggle against a relentless nature, our aim to secure as much as we can to nourish our own existence. It is even easier today, amid western affluence to see our role as a ceaseless struggle for status in a competitive and ruthless society. But if we credit the assertion that our existence is basically rooted in a reality which is both affirmative and responsive in relation to us, then the pattern of our days is different. In the first case, every moment of our waking hours which is not devoted to the struggle is to that extent wasted and irrelevant. But in the second, we shall recognise that our lives do not consist entirely of so lonely and desperate an undertaking. And it will be natural to spare time for contemplating the good nature of that affirmative and responsive environment; for personal relations which typify that sort of 'being at home in the universe'; and for the activities of thanksgiving and worship which are appropriate to the situation. In this sense the sabbath 'rules' warn against the absorption of our attention in one part only of our environment, and that perhaps the least exciting. They are a reminder of the whole range and scope of what it means to be a man, not just an animate machine. But if those rules be taken legalistically, then they actually contradict their original purpose and act as a device for emphasising the impersonal and mechanistic side of life. So it was that Jesus insisted on healing a sick man on the sabbath in full public view, a man whose illness was obviously not of such a kind that there was any urgency about his cure. And he did so in order to make clear the real nature of the maxims of Israel about the use of one day in seven. If the seventh day was intended to give time for that relationship with neighbour and Being which alone renders life truly personal, what better way of acting than to heal a man on such a day? And what greater denial of all that the sabbath stood for than to pass by a human need without attending to it?

If the Law of Israel is therefore not to be simply equated with a set of principles for right action, if it does not fit neatly the scheme of those who think in terms of law and legality, does it approximate in any degree to the position of those who judge what is right in terms of the ideal purpose our actions serve? Does the Old Testament at any point suggest that Israel is called to a campaign of human betterment, a struggle to achieve some nobler dispensation of human affairs, and that this calling should determine the style of her behaviour? The answer is revealing in its ambiguity. For the prospect which began to fill the minds of the prophets and teachers of Israel, at first chiefly concentrated on securing living space and then on the tasks of nation-building, was of a day of divine intervention. If there was anything which Israel could do to hasten this, it was simply to achieve a more perfect faithfulness to God's commands. The painful scrupulousness of the Pharisees has to be understood as an expression of this kind of devotion. The great day of intervention was often thought of chiefly as the moment of Israel's vindication before her enemies, but the really significant perceptions about it came from a few men recognised as prophets, from the eighth century BC onwards. They redefined the coming great day as one in which Israel might by no means enjoy herself in so far as it would reveal her fatal faults, and one in which all the nations of the world might participate in both judgement and salvation. But the redefinition did not alter the conviction that the event in prospect was not just the end term in a process of human historical endeavour, but some new initiative from outside history itself, a messianic age.

A closer study of the preoccupations of the prophets tends to confirm and expand some of the conclusion already adumbrated in considering the meaning of the Torah. The attempt to describe them as great moral legislators involves using categories which do not strictly belong to them. Indeed a real appreciation of their outstanding contribution to human insight had to wait till men were prepared to understand and take very seriously the historical context of their messages. For they were people whose teaching and preaching were inextricably bound up with what they saw happening around them. It was a supreme example of the demands of 'responsible action', understood as finding the fitting thing to do in a situation in which the hard facts were rigorously evaluated and their meaning deeply perceived. It could be said that the distinguishing feature of the deliverances of the prophets was a relentless realism about the political and social events of the time, in contradiction of those who wanted to utter soft and soothing words—this, coupled with an exhilarating conviction that the historical process itself had meaning and was moving in a significant direction towards a tremendous consummation. In both respects they left a lasting mark on human thought. But the second, the sense of history moving to a climax, is more truly unique and may well be the seed from which has grown the contemporary world of historical endeavour and science, all that is so often falsely condemned as materialism and which in reality arises from taking seriously and hopefully the only experience we have, our life on earth.

To try to deduce from the prophets an abstract ethical code is to miss the point, and to land in perplexity. It would be possible to cite Isaiah as a militarist urging King Ahaz not to be browbeaten by the threats of little upstarts abusing him from beneath the walls of Jerusalem (Isaiah 7. 1-9). Or alternatively, in his assessment of the significance of the rise of Assyria, and the impossibility of Israel withstanding so tremendous a threat, he could be recruited in the ranks of the 'war is senseless' brigade (Isaiah 10. 5-6). Jeremiah could devote himself to the agonising task of preparing his people for their disastrous defeat and exile, and yet purchase a plot of land to signify his view that this was not going to be the end of the story (Jeremiah 32. 6-15). The case for condemning the sophisticated extravagance of the upper set in Israel was made out by Amos not in terms of concepts of justice or laws of equality, but in terms of the fundamental nature of the situation, of how people should behave appropriately who stood in a certain relation with Yahweh and had been treated by him in such and such a way (Amos 1. 6-16). Half the time the prophets were really simply reciting again to their nation the tale of how they had been handled by their God, and calling them to remember and respond fittingly, in the new circumstances of the time. It would indeed be hard to find more perfect examples of the thesis that the judgement of right action springs not from abstract principles or devotion to noble causes but from existential awareness of the meaning of current events, realistically apprehended. Right action is that which relates one fittingly to what is going on, and to the God who is the transcendent actor in the whole situation—this is the message of the prophets. They conceived of the historical consummation which they eagerly proclaimed, against all the fatalism, cyclical concepts of history, or mysticism of surrounding religions, as an inevitable event to which men did well to adjust themselves lest they be overwhelmed by it when it came. This was the way they thought of the matter, rather than in terms of the reward of human endeavour. In our own times, however, we have to remember that it is not enough for anyone who wants to be faithful to that tradition simply to echo their perception. He must consider, too, whether in our day new and equally startling discoveries are not to be made by people who attend with the same respect to contemporary history, and bring as profound a religious insight to its interpretation.

The Law and the Prophets agreed in sounding some of the greatest notes in describing the human condition. They established the extraordinary status of men in the universe (at least so far as the men were Israelites—the greatest went always beyond to a complete universalism). Men were beings to whom God talked as companions. Or in the more abstract terms of our modern minds, men stand to ultimate being in a genuinely personal relation. The 'I—Thou' relation is not confined to human relationships but is the secret of our relation to the source of all being. And moreover, the character of that relation, determined not by us but by him in whom we live, move and have our being, is, in the archaic words of our Old Testament, tender mercy and lovingkindness. All the hard words and warnings are reserved for those who act as though their fellows were things and not people, or who, being the recipients of lovingkindness, respond to their neighbours with contradictory hostility or ruthlessness. The source of such aberrations is invariably identified as that capacity of the human heart deliberately to forget its real circumstances, and indulge in dangerous self-induced fantasies. The cure is to return to recognition of the one God of Israel and all that he has done.

There is one specific lesson to be drawn from the prophetic tradition which is worth noting before we pass on. In the international political debate it is sometimes the habit to contrast the 'realists' and the 'moralists', and the contrast may in our day have some justification. The Old Testament prophets would have had to perform most complex mental contortions even to begin to understand what such a contrast could conceivably mean. For them, a great part of the battle was to arouse the men of their day to a rigorous realism, not least in regard to international affairs. No Churchill was more pertinacious nor full of foreboding than they, nor less welcomed in calling for the recognition of what was emerging among the nations. Far from taking an optimistic view of human affairs, they found themselves urging that men should learn to tremble before the real dangers rather than the trifles which tended to engage their attention. And their concern was to discern a meaning in these dangers and dooms, one which made them tolerable, or which indicated a light at the end of a very disagreeable tunnel. There was none of the assurance that if you treat others nicely they will reciprocate, and sometimes little hope that the impending events could be diverted by a new devotion to morality. True, the plea for repentance was heard, with the suggestion that only such a radical act could change the future. But more and more this promise was cast, not in terms that by repenting men could avoid suffering, but that thereby they could pass through and beyond it to a consummation dimly seen but firmly anticipated. The contrast of 'realist' and 'moralist' does not fit into this frame. Indeed the prophets would no doubt complain of the realist that he is realistic over rather a narrow segment of the whole environment and is content as a rule to be remarkably sentimental or agnostic about some of the most significant bits. The moralist, one fears, would receive a lecture on the hard facts of history, accepted and discerned with clear-eyed acumen by those remarkable men of old.

This is the background against which to understand the teaching of Jesus Christ. The popular notion that his originality consists primarily in his superseding the cruel and primitive savageries of the Old Testament teaching with a new, idealistic ethic of love finds no support in the only serious evidence we possess, the text of the Bible itself. Enough has been said about the preoccupations of the Jewish prophets to dispel one part of such an assertion. But as to the other part, several criticisms are necessary. For one thing it is hard to find anything which one might term idealistic, in the starry-eyed sense of the word, in the records of the Gospel. Instead there is the familiar austere political realism which we have noted as a characteristic of the prophets. No-one saw more clearly than Jesus the coming fate of Jewish nationalism, or bemoaned with greater anguish the human suffering its ultimate suppression would entail. No-one more bleakly perceived the political consequences of his own teaching, or foresaw the fate likely to face those who associated themselves with his mission. People who sought his company had to be warned that it was likely to involve carrying a cross before the end.

Again, Jesus himself expressly disavowed any intention of ethical originality and wanted people to understand that his was a fulfilment rather than a contradiction of the tradition of his people. But evidently he struck his hearers as saying something new in this respect and we must identify what it was. We may sum it up by the assertion that Jesus attacked every interpretation of morality which was merely legalistic in favour of an emphasis altogether on the quality of personal relationships. What one did to another was not of itself the question at issue but how one's entire person was related to his entire person. To avoid hitting him over the head was not the point; the real fault lay in estrangement and hostility as a pattern of relation. In terms of the earlier argument of this book, Jesus was demanding a recognition that the reality to which we are called to respond is ultimately personal, and that the pattern of relationship proper to that reality has to be reflected and worked out in all other relations with our fellow human beings. The over-riding criterion for judging our actions is neither a set of rules, like those relating to sabbath-keeping or dealing with Samaritans, such as had been elaborated by the Jewish teachers; nor is it the acceptance of some noble project in history, such as the liberation of the Jewish nation. It is the here-and-now relationship offered to men by the Father. Our behaviour must be governed by the requirement to act fittingly to that relationship. The description of that relationship is the clue of the whole of life. It provides the frame and interpretation for all other human experience. It does not excuse us from assessing accurately all the factors in a problem, nor provide a short-cut past that wearisome grappling with the recalcitrant realities of the world which makes up so much of the work of political decision. But as an apparently trite musical theme is woven by a composer into the texture of a whole symphony and thereby is heard in a completely fresh way, so the mundane calculations of political reality are accorded new dimensions when seen in this proper context.

Before attempting to sketch some of the main features of that relationship to which we here refer, we must deal however briefly with the objection that if Jesus did not present a new ethic, he at least offered a new hope in the form he termed 'the kingdom of God'. Much of the misunderstanding occasioned by this phrase stems again from linguistic difficulties. Put the phrase back into the Hebrew where it was born, and at once it is clear that the emphasis, as between the two nouns, has got reversed. In English, the emphasis is on 'kingdom,' with the suggestions of territory, organisation, a community governed by a king; and from there it is simple to imagine that Jesus was talking about some kind of coming utopia in which perfection would be realised. But for the Jew the emphasis is the other way around, and it is God whose activity is declared. What is said is that it is God who rules, not in some distant future but now, and particularly by intruding upon the scene of history the person of Jesus Christ. Two quotations, dealing negatively and positively with this matter, may make the point.

We conclude that on the historical plane there is no 'eschatology of bliss' in the sayings of Jesus. He gave no promise that the future would bring with it any such perfection of human society as some Jewish thinkers had predicted under the form of a restored Kingdom of David. He declared that the Kingdom of God had come. When he spoke of it in terms of the future, his words suggest, not any readjustments of conditions on earth, but the glories of a world beyond this.[2]

If we ask what is this kingdom of God that so dominates the life and words of Jesus and rides roughshod over established belief and practice, challenging all constituted authorities, the only answer is that it is the realisation of God's will in the world.... What then is this will of God? For Pharisaic Judaism it was holiness and righteousness as revealed in the Law. For those Jews who nourished their souls on the Apocalyptic literature, there was added an intenser assurance of a Divine power that would destroy evil and vindicate righteousness, and that right early. For many the Kingdom of God meant the downfall of Rome and the exaltation of Israel to world-dominion. For Jesus the will of God is primarily the forgiving, reconciling, redeeming love of God. And being what it is, it must express itself in a divine act for men rather than in a Divine demand upon men; though this demand follows inevitably upon the act.[3]

[2] C. H. Dodd, *Parables of the Kingdom* (London: Nisbet, 1955), p. 74.
[3] T. W. Manson, *The Sayings of Jesus* (London: SCM Press, 1949), pp. 344-5.

dr 'Promise e Fulfilment'; künnel. for a different interp.

The Kingdom of God is first and foremost an act of God, and ultimately the Christians came to see that in a supreme sense Jesus himself was the Kingdom in reality. The good news of an ultimate relationship precedes any moral demands and indeed is their ground and base. The good news of Jesus Christ is not about some future prospect but primarily about an existing relationship, one brought into being and made possible by Jesus Christ himself. It will indeed have repercussions in history, sometimes acting like a general fermentation in human affairs, sometimes like a bomb, often attracting fanatical resistance and bringing all kinds of trouble on those associated with it. How it will all turn out in the end is less important than that we should be true to it now. All this is to be found in the preaching of the Kingdom of God. It is a rather long way away from the secular utopianisms that men find easier to adopt.

But J.C. spoke of the future coming of, kingdom!

If, then, we seek in the Christian tradition those resources of wisdom and insight which human beings need to find the way to peace on earth, we can now identify more clearly where to look. We are not absolved in this from the human duty to reach, by every means at our disposal, a right assessment of the human facts of the situation and a correct forecast of the likely consequences of various possible courses of action. But we are made aware that, as well as relating ourselves intelligently to all the realities we can thus discern, we have a more fundamental response to make to the whole situation, one which is in conformity with the underlying reality of our lives, the relationship we have been offered to that which is ultimate. And it is in the description of that relationship, rather than in any fixed and static set of principles, that we find the enduring criteria of what is right. Only a sketch is here possible of the chief features of that relationship.

In the first place, the biblical tradition is that God addresses men. The relationship is one in which men are treated as responsible, capable in principle of entering into a fully personal relation with God. We have already noted the fact that they thus possess a status in the universe entirely their own. We must also recognise that if the divine approach is best described as speech, this suggests a curious delicacy, as though God were concerned to preserve the conditions of voluntary response, of conversation rather than of command and obedience. Indeed in this can be seen a reason for the enigma of the hiddenness of the divine, which at first makes our minds disbelieve. For evidently, as in human relations, a true dialogue is unimaginable when a difference in status is not only great but emphasised. This thread is to be found all through the biblical testimony, the more impressive in that it is taken as axiomatic. But obviously it reaches a new intensity in any idea that, to pursue the conversation, the divine takes human form. If on the side of God the relationship is pursued with this degree of relentless patience, and one may say humility, in order to protect the human capacity for free response, we find an aspect that has immense consequences in our political concern for human freedom. In our attempt to reflect appropriately on this quality in the very nature of the human condition, we shall be driven far.

We may begin with the necessary emphasis this gives to religious freedom, and the rejection of all human attempts to go about the business of religion in another fashion. Clearly the individual's response to God is one which no man has any right to try to compel, if God does not. Of course there are more tangled issues where the solution is less obvious, not least those connected with the religious element in public institutions and activities, where the argument is interwoven with another, concerning the right balance between the rights of the individual and those of the community of which he is a part. It becomes further enmeshed in considerations as to how far political institutions and the communal activities which they sponsor should ever attempt to determine issues of ultimate meaning—a matter to be referred to in a later chapter. But at least at this stage we can appreciate the connexion between our understanding of one aspect of our relation to God and the kind of behaviour it entails for us.

Here too is the ground for much wider freedoms, and indeed it is to be insisted that they all belong together. For our political institutions must also tend in the direction of recognising the citizen as responsible in this ultimate sense. This does not mean that every man must have the right, or the illusion that he exercises the right, to handle the levers of government personally. There is so much hypocrisy necessarily talked about democracy that it is increasingly difficult to get a serious discussion about what on earth we are striving for in our devotion to this general concept. The way to show our respect for the responsibility of all our neighbours is not necessarily to establish the principle of majority rule (which can represent a fundamental contempt for the responsibility of those in the minority), nor to adopt a particular type of parliamentary mechanism or behaviour. It is to spread decision-making as widely as possible, and to exercise every sort of ingenuity to compel those with power to use it for the general good rather than to exploit others to their own advantage. The answers will not be found in any book of rules, and may vary from place to place and time to time. What is needed is the political creativity and skill to work out solutions of practical value which take serious account of this insight into the nature of reality.

Implied in the first statement about the relationship in which we stand to God is another which must be referred to separately. It is that the intention of God in addressing us is to affirm our right to life. It is this which is contained in the concept that God is love. It does not imply that we have thereby been given a right to any sort of life we fancy, but rather that we are offered life as God himself has it, which is a rather different thing, and more costly. From this may be derived our understanding of the burgeoning of our mastery of the natural world, not of itself any guarantee of our felicity but the condition on which we can reach a full humanity. From it too can be better understood the historical developments which throw all of us humans together in mutuality, so that we cannot escape the challenge of each other's needs. For all this is the life of God.

We can see with some certainty particular political developments which have no conceivable future in this context. An attempt to deprive sections of the human community of this possibility of response to life, because of some features of race or culture, simply has no future. Nor do those who shrink from the perils of our enlarged knowledge and capacities and deplore the passing of our human childhood and adolescence, have any real hope of retarding these developments. Human beings are all

68

equally addressed by God, although infinitely various in their capacities, and this fact must be reflected in our human institutions. We are all together being drawn into new realms of responsibility, and there is no way of halting the providential process.

The third feature of our relationship to the divine which is exhibited in the biblical tradition concerns forgiveness. Here something must first be said to make the point itself understandable. We are well aware in international politics of the two conflicting modes of reaction. One is a growing sense of human solidarity, of the simple fact that we cannot escape involvement in each other's business, of the necessity to give this sense of unity formal and institutional articulation. On the other hand, we live at a time when men are particularly prone to define the issues which divide us in moral terms. The act of condemnation—of tyranny, race oppression, social injustice—puts us at one stroke at a distance from the object of our scorn. The very intention is to dissociate ourselves from what we believe to be wrong. There is an inescapable element of self-righteousness about it, however loud our protests of humility. So we reach the point where the two modes of reaction seem directly contradictory, and the only way we can affirm our solidarity is by suppressing our indignation, in a pallid form of co-existence; and the only way we can express the seriousness of our moral feeling is at the risk of disrupting such human community as we have on this earth.

The relationship we are offered in the gospel is one which takes this dilemma with great profundity and greater compassion. For the one who addresses us is not blind to those elements in our nature which render us unfit for his company. The terms of his judgement upon us are not however estranging. By his own device he puts himself immediately beside us even while he judges, and insists on carrying the consequences of that judgement himself, with us. Here is a fundamental aspect of the matter that helps us to see how judgement is expressed in the affairs of men. We are right to recognise the intolerable for what it is, but we may not condemn it until we too are able to share the burden of its condemnation. By this one stroke that most dangerous of international moods, the mood of apparently justified righteous condemnation of other nations and societies, is radically called in question. A means is discovered whereby we can begin to bring together a realistic judgement, and human solidarity. It is a way which is most disconcerting in its cost. To condemn the sins of the world is easy and will be widely acclaimed as 'outspoken' and 'courageous.' To hesitate because of a doubt about one's own status as a judge is understandable and can be noble. But to put oneself alongside that which we condemn, and bear the condemnation without abating the judgement, is going to hurt and isolate in an expensive way.

This, we may add, is the objective ground for the elaboration of those aspects of the doctrine of the Just War which attempt to limit violence. Men are always tempted to believe that once it comes to war, total estrangement has taken place and no obligations remain between the contestants. The episode of the crucifixion of Jesus provides us with the indispensible clue for the assertion that, however profound our hostility to another nation or society or however necessary it may be to resist its policies, we remain tied in a human solidarity with our enemy. Thus we may never contemplate total war or his liquidation, nor even the destruction of his society.

Sometimes Christians have argued concerning the mode of the death of Jesus that here was a new technique for overcoming resistance to what one conceived to be good. From this is developed a whole philosophy of international behaviour. But surely there is a sort of blasphemy in interpreting this act of sacrifice in terms of practical techniques, of devices to get one's own way in the end at whatever cost. There is, at any rate, little in the New Testament itself to suggest such a notion. Instead the crucifixion of Jesus is interpreted solely in terms of our human relation to our Father, as an act utterly appropriate to the truth of that relationship, at once exposing our alienation and at the same time overcoming it.

Can't it also be an act 'utterly appropriate' to each individual's relationship with God?

4

CHRISTIANITY AND POWER

W E N O W H A V E available a fuller understanding of what we
mean when we define right action as that which is a serious and
fitting response to—or stage in the continuing dialogue with—
our environment. Such a definition could conceivably refer to the
mindless adjustments which form part of the process of natural
evolution. But within the Christian tradition the dialogue with
the environment is understood fundamentally as 'personal encounter'. Behind and within every option or choice of policy
there is an offer of a personal relation at the deepest level, to be
accepted or rejected. To interpret the meaning of events which
demand our answering decisions, it is contended that we have to
see them as part of the activity of ultimate being, disclosing
himself throughout the history recorded and interpreted in the
Bible, but supremely in Jesus Christ. And here we have, not only
as it were a message from beyond or within our ordinary experience, but also the supremely fitting human response, made
on behalf of the human race.

A number of very important consequences flow from this. To
begin with it elevates the characteristically human to the
supreme place in our estimation. The crucial area of concern for
mankind, in finding the right action and making the fitting responses, lies not in the development of man's mastery over the
world of nature, nor in his exploration of the world of aesthetics
and of art, nor in the enlargement of his knowledge and capacity
for appreciation. All these activities are given their proper significance only in a universe where the ultimate issues are in the
sphere of personal relations, thus reflecting the fundamental relation in which we stand to our environment. For this reason

politics, and not least international politics, where the relations of great groups of persons to one another are ordered and given some sort of coherence and meaning, are rightly felt to present major challenges to our decision. It is not so much that the Christian tradition supplies us with a code of rules for working out such relationships in ever-changing circumstances. Rather it is an account of how such a relationship was worked out over centuries from God's side, through all the variants and vicissitudes of a long history. This gives us an insight into what genuine personal relations are like, what it is to enter into truly personal relationship with other human beings.

For instance, the divine offer of relationship does not appear to have been controlled by any estimate of intrinsic worth. The Jewish leaders could never see anything particularly remarkable about their nation which could have led to their being 'chosen'. Whatever they understood by 'tender mercy and lovingkindness' as attributes of God, it appears to have included decisively a fundamental respect for a man's right to be—expressed in God's readiness to address human beings in fully personal terms and to wait upon their answer. And it was one of the great breaks-through of the New Testament to realise that God's address had no racial or national limitation, but was to human beings as such. In terms of modern international politics this has considerable significance. It means that a somewhat different slant is given to issues of racial equality or national self-determination We are not burdened with the hopeless task of defining what we mean by the equality of all men. By any criteria we know of, the proposition is not true, and a lot of nonsense flows from attempts to assert it, including a refusal to recognise human excellence where it does emerge. But if each human being, with all the limitations of his inherited equipment, the culture in which he was reared, or the ugly history of which he is heir, is by reason of his humanity respectfully invited to personal encounter with ultimate reality, and his personal response is treated as important, this gives him a status which it behoves his fellows to recognise. It is beyond the reach of human criticism.

Of course this does not involve a romantic view of our human nature—quite the contrary. The very notion of personal encounter carries the implication of an indeterminate outcome, awaiting the decision of the parties to the encounter. So that a proper understanding of the drama of human life, of our critical response to the challenges which present themselves, involves a full recognition that our response may be negative, destructive, hostile or blind. Those who understand men's capacity for making war or oppressing one another as solely the result of environmental factors do less than justice to the extra-ordinary beings they are dealing with. In appearing to excuse man from responsibility for these things they in fact diminish his stature as a responsible being. Certainly we must do everything possible to create an environment in which war and oppression are discouraged, and this will be the area of consideration in later chapters. But to understand ourselves and our neighbours in the light of the Christian tradition is to take very seriously our capacity for choosing wrong. The reasons we give for promoting self-determination and enlarging human freedom are not that thereby we provide conditions in which war becomes less likely, but that this is the only truly fitting response to the nature of the reality confronting us, and we must deal with the consequences as they emerge.

These examples serve to illustrate the way in which the Christian tradition impinges on the international scene. It is not an attempt to introduce a set of static rules to be imposed with some degree of casuistry on the infinitely varied experiences of history. Such rules can more readily commend themselves as having some sort of eternal validity in times when the changes in society are slow and invisible, so that responses learnt from a previous generation do well enough for their children. How much of the conventional bewailing of the decay of moral values is in reality a bewailing that the moral questions to be answered are no longer the familiar ones. In truth the rapidly changing nature of our modern societies forces us to a more dynamic approach to our moral problems, and one which leaves far more room for originality, creativity and imaginative construction.

Again, the Christian tradition does not contribute by adding to, or contradicting, the facts already before us on which a judgement must be based—certainly not if we interpret facts in scientific terms. Nor does it call in question the importance of getting the relevant facts correctly stated. Rather it is at the inevitable point of interpreting the significance of facts, and discerning meaning and coherence in them, that Christian faith does its proper work. For its consequence is to set the problem in a context of meaning which gives particular priority to certain facts over others, and alters our appreciation of their significance. The immutable element is what we know of the personal relation offered to us in Jesus—what the nature and quality of the relationship is. This relationship is one which is constantly offered to us, not on our terms but on his, in every choice we make; and the essential term is that the decisions we make reflect the relationship we are offered. There is room here for endless novelty, as the subject matter of our decision varies with the pace of history. What remains unchanging is the character of the personal encounter, and of the personal relationship offered in Jesus Christ, with all that it imposes by way of obligation to live in accordance with such a relationship.

But does not the Christian faith also promise that those who live by the truth will find new methods and techniques which will produce desired results in human affairs? This is an idea with a long and respectable history, not least in the Bible. Is it not true that good fortune will be the consequence of righteous living, and that prosperity, or achieving one's good purposes, will follow obedience to the commandments of God? In part the Book of Job was the developed answer of the Old Testament to that over-simplification. But undoubtedly the scandal of the crucifixion was the final word. There is in the Christian gospel no simple promise of historical victory associated with the way of Jesus Christ, and plenty of warnings of the certainty of suffering and rejection. Thus an end is firmly set to the notion of religion as an esoteric magic formula for getting what you want. The Christian faith offers no short-cuts of that kind—only direction over the long haul. But there is one respect in which the light of the Christian faith can illuminate new courses of action. It is certainly true that an understanding of the real conditions of human life, coupled with a deep identification with the human predicament, can suggest hypotheses for experimental testing, which would in principle be accessible to other minds. And once proved they could be generally accepted without religious presuppositions. It was a profoundly Christian mind which conceived the possibility that human affairs could be conducted without slavery, which people down the centuries had accepted as inevitable (and of course also convenient). The rehabilitation of social misfits, the possibility of taking seriously the mentally deranged, are human activities today which have benefited from the scientific research and skill of men of many convictions, but where originally some important initiatives arose amongst those who were convinced about the status of such rejected human beings in the sight of God.

Here the most difficult controversies arise within the Christian community itself. Which of the facts of the situation are we to take at their face value, and which are subject to substantial re-interpretation in the light of Christian conviction? What sort of political 'realism' is proper to Christian thinking? Evidently, an interpretation of the human condition which explicitly or implicitly denied the primacy of personal relations or conceived of them solely in terms of rivalry and the struggle to dominate would be in Christian terms a completely misleading account of the facts. But what recognition are we to give to the interplay of power in human affairs, and its conscious regulation? Or are we as Christians committed to the elimination of power as a factor in favour of the relationships of love? The rest of this chapter will be devoted to elucidating this question, for it lies at the root of many fruitless arguments.

The case for recruiting the Christian forces on the side of those who want to eliminate the factor of power in human relationships is based on the disclosure by Jesus Christ of a response of suffering and passion to the evil forces directed against him. By his way of living and the particular manner of his death, we are led to see an inescapable element in the personal encounter of men with God. One who is by definition Almighty is represented as washing the feet of his friends. One who is apparently wholly without self-seeking is represented as letting himself be executed by the proud and confident religious and political forces of his time. Patience, forgiveness, the most costly self-expenditure— these are for ever declared to be essential elements in God's relation to us, and by logical analogy the only real basis for relations between men. Therefore, it is contended, the attempt to organise our human affairs in terms of power is a fundamental mistake, based on the illusions of darkened minds.

This understanding of Christianity has a long and curious history, but it must be admitted that it lacks any great intellectual tradition. It is very likely that whatever strength it possesses today derives from its conformity to other contemporary notions which are fashionable for quite different reasons. For the odd thing is that it seems to flourish just when the recognition and control of power has become the dominant problem in human affairs. There never was a time when men possessed such power as they do today, or had created complexes of effective power—political, technological, economic or military—as have become possible since the burgeoning of the industrial revolution. Moreover it is quite inconceivable that the process could be reversed without catastrophe. In the words of Herbert Rosinski:

> Power of every conceivable kind has been developing on a scale that staggers the imagination; yet we have remained most reluctant to draw the inevitable conclusions. In none of the major theories of society and politics of the last two centuries have the problems posed by this tremendous build-up of energies in industrial mass societies been adequately recognised. They have no place in the ideology of Western democracy, which is still thinking mainly in the terms of the eighteenth century Enlightenment and the Manchester School. They were only very partially recognised by Hegel, because he thought mainly in the political terms of the French Revolution. Nor were they recognised by Marx, who similarly turned away from the reality of power in order to dream of a power-free, world-wide 'society of free men'. Whatever our intellectual heritage, all of us have preferred in greater or lesser degree to ignore the realities of power and the problems of recognition and control with which it confronts us. Instead, we have indulged in day-dreams of an increasingly power-free world that would be freed from all concern with this most decisive and challenging aspect of our existence.[1]

[1] Herbert Rosinski, *Power and Human Destiny* (London: Pall Mall Press, 1965), p. 15. This book, posthumously published, represents the brilliant summary by his friend Richard Stebbins of the massive notes left behind by Herbert Rosinski. It is, in the opinion of the present writer, a contribution to the understanding of the technological world into which we are moving which deserves much wider attention than it has so far received. Much of the thought of the present chapter has been at least stimulated by Rosinski's perception.

There can be no serious argument about the fact that Christians in some numbers have aided and abetted this confusion, sometimes by taking the prejudices and delusions of the age and simply supplying them with theological justification.

The prejudices of the age are themselves more easily understood. The development of the industrial revolution by private initiative in the West became an absorbing occupation, and people imagined that it depended on preventing power of one sort or another interfering with free initiative. They did not see that the process itself was rapidly creating new *foci* of power—great industrial organisations, trades unions, financial complexes—which had their own empires of a sort. Karl Marx was bitterly resented when, with profound insight, he set about exposing the great new power factors at work in industrial society. But he was a product of the old pre-industrial world in so far as he could imagine that the phase of great power concentrations was a temporary one, and that it would lead eventually to a society more like the powerless pre-industrial world of old. The modern concept of democracy seemed to offer the prospect that political power would be widely dispersed throughout society. It was not easy at first to perceive that in a mass society the individual would cease to count unless he were part of a particular group, a party, a trades union, a member of a farmers' organisation or consumers' group, each representing new experiments in the concentration of effective power. And finally in the emerging nations, power had been experienced in recent times almost entirely in the form of imperial alien control on the political plane, or the invasion of foreign industrial forces on the economic plane, so that liberation could be conceived as a release from power in such forms. For the time being, therefore, they inevitably underestimate the problem of controlling and using power and will be forced by the myths of the colonial period to conceal from themselves the extent to which power remains an essential factor in the life of society.

In what way, then, are Christian perceptions related to this world of power? We might begin to reply by acknowledging that the concept of a fitting response, which we have found a useful one in searching for guidance in making right choices, itself implies power. For only when we have the capacity to affect

77

events one way or another do we have responsibility to make a
real choice. And as soon as we have the capacity to affect events,
we have power. The startling feature of the modern world is the
enormous increase in our capacity to choose what will happen.
If at the same time, we are seeing an increasing listlessness and
withdrawal from the task of making such choices, may it not be
because the presuppositions with which we are working conceal from us the tools of power which we have to use to make our
choices real and effective? It is all too easy to hide a certain
timidity of spirit and congenital ineffectiveness behind an apparent disavowal of the power factor in human affairs.

But we must still answer the basic question—if the fundamental relation in which we stand is one of personal encounter
with the God who is the source and substance of all our existence, and if he has shown that this personal relation demands
absolutely a readiness to bear the sins of another rather than
defeat him by the exercise of power against his will, what conceivable guidance can we get from this in facing the realities of
power in modern society? The answer is surely to be sought, not
by trying to demolish the plain facts of experience, but by asking
how they can be used, controlled and manipulated so that they
serve the ends of such a personal relation. We are living in a
world where there has always been power of a sort, in many
different forms, but one in which men are now daily developing
powers and power-institutions on a scale quite unprecedented.
The relations of men to each other have always been in part
personal, but also and inevitably in part impersonal. In modern
mass society impersonal relationships predominate. I do not
know who it is who connects my telephone to that of my
relations so that we can have a very personal conversation. The
factors at work to bring to my table a cup of cocoa are far outside my detailed knowledge and involve people I shall never
meet. In such impersonal relationships we can see those in which
power factors are decisive. The cost of my telephone call depends
on the wages of the operator whom I do not know, and the wages
are fixed not by personal encounter but by the resolution of a
complex series of influences in which political and economic
and social power groups play a substantial part. Whether or not
I can afford a cup of cocoa is decided by a whole marketing

apparatus which is subject to pressures and forces even beyond those of a single nation. But the attempt to secure a just system of wages and reasonable terms of employment, or to control the market forces so that the cocoa-producer is not exploited—these are activities which can only be effectively pursued by candid recognition of the power factors at play and by the resolve to master them for human ends. On the success of doing so depends realistically my capacity to reach a genuine personal relation with my neighbour at home, or to achieve an honest friendship with someone from Ghana whose welfare depends on cocoa prices.

The truth of the matter is that in order to make a responsible answer to the personal encounter with God, in terms of the group activities of men, it is morally incumbent on us to take seriously the realities of the power factors in human societies. In the same way, in dealing with ill-health, we do not depersonalise or dehumanise treatment by the fact that we recognise the reality of the existence of bacteria and the blind nature of their activities in the human body, but seek by recognising such facts to control them for the benefit of men. Our distaste for political realism in this respect often springs not so much from a refined conscience as from a dislike of that aspect of the truth of things which challenges a sentimental, comfortable, and soothing view of the human condition. By refusing to take seriously the real power factors we give ourselves so false an analysis of the problem before us that we render ourselves impotent to cope with it, and instead become the victims of its autonomous operations.

A concrete issue of international affairs illustrates this point. It is the priority accorded to disarmament as an urgent objective of all good men, particularly worthy of Christian support. Indeed there can be no dispute about the mortal danger in which mankind stands while no control exists over the development and proliferation of modern armaments. The question however is whether we have defined rightly the nature of the problem so that it begins to yield to the solutions that we devise for it. For the power confrontation of nations and ideologies is represented only partly by military hardware, and would undoubtedly continue even if the hardware were all disposed of. It would seek other expressions. We can observe this happening at the present time, when the mortal danger of escalation is widely appreciated and other ways are therefore sought for pursuing conflict and rivalry—subversion, psychological warfare, economic influence and the rest. In so far as such methods succeed and begin to touch the vital interests of the nation or alliance against which they are directed, all the dangers are reactivated that a major explosion of destructive power will take place. A truer appreciation of the power factors in modern highly industrialised societies would show that it is vain to hope that our affairs will subside into a kind of tranquillity if we succeed in reducing and limiting one expression of that power, the military. The real value of negotiations about disarmament is that they cover a field where there is very substantial common interest to be explored, and a commonly understood danger to be averted—so that agreement is in principle a possibility. And the achieving of it might offer models and instruments for wider co-operation in other fields of power confrontation.

We can observe in arguments over this matter of disarmament how accurate is Rosinski's comment that while power of every conceivable kind has been developing on an unheard-of scale, all schools of thought have been most reluctant to draw the inevitable conclusions. The delusions of Western democracy meet happily with those of Marxist ideology in jointly announcing a common objective of 'general and complete disarmament'. Both sides are urged on in this direction by the emerging world, itself as yet unfamiliar with the problems of the control of modern power, and believing that what is spent on arms could and should be diverted to the economic development of the poorer countries of the world. It makes an impressive picture which cannot fail to capture the attention of the moralist. No decent person would lightly discourage such thoughts unless they were seen to distract our minds from dealing with the real problem. This is not how we rid ourselves of the monstrous power we now possess (for we can never retrace that road), but how we control it for human ends. The dream of a power-drained international order is, and ought to be honestly said to be, a total fantasy, and one which the Christian faith has no interest in propagating. Let us be accused of pessimism or lack of the necessary determination of the will—but let us avoid at all costs being party to the lazy sentimentalities and cynical double-talk which offer men hopes that have no basis in our common experience or the faith to which we are committed. Historical disaster is more likely to be caused by a preference for soothing slogans, than a rigorous determination to face reality however disconcerting.

Once it is firmly before our minds that the possibility does not really exist of dealing with the confrontation of military power by trying to organise its disappearance, we are at last free to see what the real nature of our problem is. Evidently it is to create such controls and balances that mankind can live with power of that order, and not have to fear its running amok into a general catastrophe. This is quite a different task from general and comprehensive disarmament, though it may very well involve a useful reduction in the level of arms expenditure. The argument illustrates the point of this chapter that the great problem facing the human race today is not how to find safety by abolishing or 'banning' power, but how to establish truly human control over the immense and growing powers which we are daily developing.

5

'PROGRESSIVE' GOVERNMENT

THE SECOND AREA in which men have sought the key to international peace is in the internal structure of states. In the first chapter we briefly scanned some of the sources and expositions of the idea that if states could solve their own interior conflicts and devise just and efficient systems of government within themselves, they would be no more tempted to go to war. Then we noted a few of the more obvious discrepancies in such theories, leaving to this present chapter a more detailed examination of the contemporary form of such ideas.

That contemporary form is one which judges governments according to categories related to the great changes taking place under our eyes in the social, economic and political structures of the world. Thus governments can be classified as 'progressive' or 'reactionary' according to the degree to which they are identified with the forces of change, or seek to conserve, more or less, the traditional patterns of power and culture. It is customary to go on from there, and to take it as axiomatic that progressive states will offer little threat to international order and stability, and that reactionary states will be associated closely with militarism. There is therefore a certain justification for making an exception, in terms of our ordinary duty to maintain international peace, of those cases where it is felt to be necessary to overthrow the power of a reactionary government in order that its progressive successor may come to the fore and by definition prove itself a more reliable supporter of the international community and its stability. 'Wars of liberation' are justified by such an argument.

With or without the addendum justifying 'wars of liberation', this general thesis is one which makes an appeal to all those who are truly sensitive to the human condition, who feel the intolerable burden of the *status quo* as it bears down upon the poor, the exploited, and those who are oppressed on grounds of race. Simply to settle for things as they are and imagine that peace can be maintained thereby is to reject for ever the dream of a fairer justice on earth. So there is a strong moral incentive to support policies which call themselves 'progressive', and there is sometimes an undiscriminating judgement that anything is better than what we have now. The question, however, which has to be asked in all such cases is not under what banner governments place themselves but in what direction true progress lies and which interests and powers are most likely to pursue it in that direction.

It is important therefore first to look in greater detail at the thesis that progressive governments will tend to be those which find it easiest to live at peace with their neighbours, and to analyse the reasons why this should be so. As soon as we look closely at the proposition we can detect several different notions wrapped up in it. There is first the idea that a government which is in harmony with the dynamic forces within the society which it controls will be under fewer temptations to venture into an aggressive foreign policy—either to distract internal complaints or to export political irresponsibility. This can be further elaborated by saying that progressive governments, being those which express the general will, are less and less required to think in terms of force and the instruments of compulsion, and that therefore to them the whole paraphernalia of war become increasingly alien. The argument can be taken to its logical conclusion with the Marxists who look for a day of such harmony that the state itself withers away, and mankind's universal life can be conducted entirely on a voluntary basis. Progress, as understood in this context, consists of the movement away from a conception of government which is from above downwards, and which imposes the will of the governing group on all else. It is the movement towards a state of affairs which is at least more democratic, in which government receives its authority from the governed, and increasingly becomes the public expression of the general will. It is not difficult to see that this idea has its roots rather in the more optimistic elements in the thought of the period of the European Enlightenment than in anything more modern. The disharmony which fills the picture is that between governor and governed. This is the cause of human troubles, and were it removed the human future could be anticipated as one of prosperity and peace. The question is never faced whether the mere fact that we appear, at least in present circumstances, to need government at all does not suggest other sources of disharmony of a persisting kind.

But before undertaking any systematic critique of such a point of view we should do justice first to some of the valid elements within it. We must, for instance, ask what validity attaches to the assertion that in our times reactionary regimes are a source of international unrest. There are several very important elements involved in such a view. First, it springs from the recognition that human society has entered a process of accelerating change which has no historic precedent. So far as any eye can see at this moment, there is no discernible terminus to that process nor is there any reason to suppose that the pace of change will slow. The interplay of new technologies, conferring immeasurable powers on men to master their environment, with a corresponding self-awareness and self-respect of the human person, creates a new dynamism in human affairs which no human institution can completely suffocate. Forms and philosophies of government elaborated in another age, disposing of power but no longer coherent with what is happening all around them, inevitably are sources of friction in such a human society. And friction in any part of our modern society infects in some degree the whole. No longer is it possible to isolate a troubled area from the concern of other men and women. At the same time an unpopular regime may seek to augment its prestige by outside adventures.

Archaic regimes of this kind linger on in Latin America, for instance, and represent a future menace to the peace not only of the sub-continent but of much wider areas. The need for radical change is matched by the apparent impossibility of effecting it without considerable violence. But it is important to recognise that these are not the only places where governmental systems are afflicted with rigidity. Some of the political novelties of this century already display painful inflexibilities, though of a different intensity to be sure. The USSR government, in its efforts to come to terms both with the demands of its emerging self-conscious citizens and the requirements of its rapidly elaborating economy, has been subject at times to severe strains; and the machinery for effecting substantial changes and reassessments of policy still works with creaks and groans. It is not clear how the newly emerging states will cope with the pressure of change upon their governmental institutions, but it has to be admitted that where the task of nation-building has required strong centralisation in government and the suppression of some forces of dissent, the problem of flexibility and change has been made that much harder to solve. Nor can we omit the wealthy nations of the West from the list of those who find it hard to live up to a 'progressive' label. They are not, of course, under quite so much pressure in so far as they can afford vast mistakes without disaster. But the problem of defining the proper role of central authority in the management of society, and of bringing into subservience the great vested-interest groups which are components of the party machinery of Western democracy, remains on the agenda. Of course it is true that governments subject to periodic election, where there is some degree of real choice left to the electorate, possess a regulator of change which has very considerable value. But even this operates effectively only if other features of the society are conducive to imaginative and creative political construction. To have to choose between two relatively archaic institutions is no indication of flexibility.

Thus we begin to come within sight of some criteria by which to judge what is, and what is not, 'progressive'. At this stage of the argument the word is taken to refer to the capacity of government to respond to the new and always changing demands of modern society with appropriate adjustments of its own understanding of its role, and a creative perception of the measures it must adopt to regulate the life of a modern state. Flexibility and creativity are not natural features of any great public institution, least of all perhaps the apparatus of central government. It is therefore implied in this definition that some arrangement exists to disturb, provoke, or stimulate the machinery of administration and government to alter its accustomed ways and if necessary change the management. Against such a standard many a regime which lays claim to a progressive label can do so only on the basis of one short-lived, perhaps revolutionary gesture, and must recognise in due course the difficulty of maintaining the momentum. Yet there is no secure resting-place today, once a community has set its feet on the path of change.

But there is something important missing from such a definition of 'progressive'. We use the term to mean something more morally admirable and humane than simple flexibility would suggest. Part of the process of change which we recognise as marking, in some sense universally, the evolution of human history at this juncture, is men's new awareness of themselves, their worth and dignity, and their claims upon the common resources of mankind. It is not so much a new insight, for it has had its place in all the noblest records of human thought and understanding, perhaps supremely enshrined in the scriptures of the Jewish people. What is new is the recognition of its universal application. In those long centuries when the struggle to survive demanded of all but the privileged few a form of existence 'nasty, brutish and short', it required the eye of religious faith to recognise the significance of faceless men. But nowadays—when each man can dispose of some appreciable fraction of economic demand, when he is no longer required to sell his labour to whoever would feed him, and he possesses a margin of time and energy beyond what is needed to keep his family alive—then he is in some sort of position to command the recognition which before was accorded only as an act of faith and grace. This fundamental and critical element in our interpretation of what is happening to the human race, supremely in the latter half of the twentieth century, adds depth to what we mean when we condemn a regime as archaic. It is not only that at a time of tremendous developments it is manifesting an incapacity to adjust to technical and political realities. The real gravamen of the condemnation is that it is blind to the new self-consciousness of men. Whereas the classical justification of governmental activity has been that in some sense it represented transcendent authority over against the common man, now it must learn to justify itself in terms of the service it renders to the community at large. The eclipse of the idea of divine right attaching to political authorities has been going on for a long time but the full nature of that revolution in human thought has yet to be universally appreciated. It is a feature of the era of man's coming of age.

This is the context in which the word 'progressive' has real emotive power, to the ends of the earth. For everywhere the spirit stirs which insists that government is not something which has a sort of validity of its own, but that its justification and necessity is to be sought in terms of the welfare of the human community. Anti-colonialism, racial revolt, the welfare state, the universal if sometimes somewhat formal obeisance made to the concept of democracy, are all versions of the same human assertion *vis-à-vis* government that it must be stripped of all pretensions other than the duty to serve and uphold the welfare of the people. Under this classification a government is reactionary which continues to maintain a paternalistic posture in relation to its citizens, however persuasively it can argue that the resulting state of affairs is beneficial. For what is at issue is not simply a pragmatic judgement as to what type of governmental machinery will most efficiently deliver the goods, but the question of the status of men in relation to government itself. It is important to recognise that at this particular moment of history the burning issues are more often about matters of human status than economic welfare, and that economic welfare becomes an issue of consequence in great measure as a symbol and manifestation of status.[1]

---

[1] This of course is not to belittle the human problem of starvation and need. But the wealthy world is easily tempted to imagine that if people are provided with the essential requirements for life they can be persuaded to live quietly, even if they are put in an inferior position politically, racially or nationally. The problem of the underdeveloped world is in no small part a question of how the great bulk of mankind can be given a say in how the world is run, and the job not left exclusively to the few and the white.

One of the characteristic contributions of the Bible, and noticeably of the teaching and actions of Jesus, has been to divorce wealth and status from each other. The great Christian teaching about poverty contains two elements; that economic strength, which is not of itself to be condemned, confers no special status but rather that status attaches to the poor precisely because they are vulnerable and need protection; and secondly, that wealth is not intrinsically to be rejected but represents, in its temptations, a most serious danger to the real riches of life which consist in the quality of personal relations with all men, specially those in need.

Such a deflation of governmental pretensions, particularly when it occurs in societies of rapid economic expansion, can combine with a mood of optimism and euphoria to suggest that we are on the way to the time when we can perhaps eliminate this also from among the frustrations that have limited our free expression of ourselves—that the day will come when government can be reduced to a minimum, and that meanwhile virtue will lie in its doing as little as possible of what might be considered unpopular. This is no doubt one of the reasons why elements of old-fashioned liberalism of the Manchester School variety still sprout and flourish in the alien soil of the modern world. The preoccupation of 'all good men and true' of those days was to define and limit the powers of central government, to check the arrogance of those in authority, and to enlarge the area of free co-operation in the happy assurance that left to themselves men would discover the natural harmonies of their interests and relationships. Something of that mood of humanistic elation finds fertile ground again in the social, racial and political revolutions of our time. For as revolutions challenge pretentious power they tend to promise the time when power itself can be dispensed with. One more heave, even if it spills blood, and we shall break though to the era when we can finally turn swords into ploughshares—such is the dream.

The question to be asked is whether progress really lies in this direction. The argument that follows indicates why in fact much of this thinking is nostalgic and in the strictest sense reactionary, and why it is unlikely to prove a contribution to the establishment of peace. We shall have to consider positively what form of 'progressivism' is more likely to serve the building up of human society in a coherent and relatively harmonious way. The key to the discussion is the recognition of the reality of power itself, and the quite unprecedented emergence of huge *foci* of power in human affairs which is an inevitable concomitant of the very technical developments which gave men a new assessment of themselves. The evolution which liberates man from being the hard-pressed play-thing of nature, at the same time creates new factors of power which threaten to enslave him, perhaps even more terribly. But the way of escape is not by succumbing to the temptation to imagine a purely mythical day when it is possible to have the advantages of plenty without the menace of the instruments which create and serve abundance. Rather it is to recognise with realism and courage the true nature of the menace and set about mastering it. Such general remarks require concrete illustration.

Take as a basic example the emergence of the industrial processes themselves, now served by inventive and creative scientific research leading to ever more complex and elaborate operations. This produces and requires industrial combines capable of developing and administering widely-spread human activities. The traditional 'progressive' criticism has been that these entities were governed by the profit-motive. On the scale of modern industry this is relatively the least significant thing about them. Far more important is the way their very existence shapes and determines the lives and circumstances of hosts of human beings, till perhaps few people remain who are not affected in one way or another by the activities of such industries. They determine the location of housing, create or disperse towns, fix the terms on which innumerable people spend most of their waking hours, and in sometimes imperceptible ways attach human lives to their machines and the demands those machines make. The whole complex is such that in extreme cases, such as the British motor industry, fifty men may have to choose between refraining from a defence of what they consider their just rights or putting tens of thousands of work-mates on the streets. Their relations to one another seem wholly determined by the complicated machinery of which they are now a part.

This is the most obvious instance of what is meant by the development of *foci* of power as an inescapable concomitant of the technological age into which we are moving so fast. Others could be sought in the field of sheer organisation where modern techniques of communication and control enable the activities of men over a wide field to be coordinated on a scale undreamt of until recently. The emperors of old could scarcely hold their uneasy dominions together; today North America functions in some respects as a single machine. Involved in the process is the elaborate art of public relations and personnel management, along with the instruments of mass communication. And as part of the necessary equipment there is the propensity to address each other in simplified, sloganised terms designed to get results rather than to establish conversation. By slow degrees it is coming to be realised that these powers which we have let loose in the world threaten us not simply because they can be wielded by sinister and selfish vested-interests, but more seriously because they often appear to operate mindlessly. Our cities grow and get congested, not because anyone decides that this should be so, but because we have not developed organs powerful and competent enough to take hold of the process itself and render it serviceable to human needs. Our shrinking from putting into human hands too much of the disposition of our affairs has the effect of leaving us the victims of blind forces.

The moral of this is that we are moving towards a state of affairs in which we shall not be able by any conceivable means to reduce the factor of power in the world, and must face the certainty that it is liable constantly to increase. This is what we mean in part by saying that mankind is coming of age. Just as the adolescent will, from time to time, revert to the old securities of childhood and irresponsibility, so men today play with fantasies of a future when we need endure the bruising or the guilt of power no more. No such day is in sight. Instead we are challenged to find the means to control and direct the great engines of power so that they remain our servants. This does not mean a future of widening liberty in the sense of a dilution of the element of central compulsive authority. Rather it promises that the part of our lives devoted to communal productivity may become shorter with the advance of automation and cybernetics, and that the setting of our existence may be more determinedly designed to be congenial to humane values.

This excursion into sociological paths permits us to survey the landscape from a position where the view is less obstructed by placards. Once we essay to draw an analogous picture of the international scene, we are in the midst of familiar controversy. For the factor of power in international relations, and its consideration in connexion with questions of peace and war, is dominated by the inevitably heated arguments over nuclear weapons. Here are the foremost symbols of our problem, representing the product of our advanced industrial technology in the realm of war, potential vehicles of untold power, mindless in

their terrible threat. The natural reaction of horror is to call for
their abolition, as though by some marvel we could denude ourselves of the capacities we have now acquired. Such a response
fits snugly with the whole aspiration for a world in which the
element of power has been once again diminished as it was in
the time of our poverty. But it is a fairy tale, and the reasons for
that judgement have often enough been rehearsed. Whether
nuclear power is latent in the form of the knowledge and instruments able to form a bomb, or overt in the existence of the manu-
factured article, is (in terms of power rather than of morality)
simply a matter of time—can the weapon be immediately de-
ployed, or does it need a short period to prepare? Were it, by
some international arrangement, suppressed, there is unfortunately nothing to prevent human ingenuity from turning to some
other type of technology to devise an alternative system of
destruction. We have got to learn to live with the fact that we are
now powerful creatures, and there is no known way of 'banning'
our power to destroy. This does not of course prejudge the
question whether at a given moment a nation should consider relinquishing its claim to nuclear power as a political contribution to some stabilisation or wider settlement. But it does
imply that whatever be the guilt and sin of knowing how to do
these things, there is no escape from them, and the angel with
the flaming sword stands at the gate of our lost Eden of
innocence and comparative impotence. Once again, the situation challenges us not to evade the consequences of attaining untold power, but resolutely to set about the task of finding means
to curb, control and master the power at our command, so that
it serves human interests rather than threatens human survival.
In this specific field it is hard to avoid the conclusion that this
means putting nuclear weapons under the control of an international authority, so designed that it cannot become the
captive of sectional, ideological or national interests. The universal community would thus become the guardian of the thing
which threatens universally.

The same process of argument would lead us to the opinion
that the search for disarmament has an importance falling a
little short of primary. Of course, the vision of a world in which
military forces have been reduced to a level just sufficient to

guard frontiers and insure internal security is not, of itself, fantastic. It is however essentially static, permitting only of such changes as can be engineered by weight of argument (a poor enough instrument in international negotiations) or by more devious ways of exerting pressure than overt threat of force. Indeed it has to be faced that the reduced capacity to exert physical pressure would tend greatly to augment the attention given to other ways of doing the same thing—the methods of subversion, propaganda, economic influence and the like. Inevitably a government seeking to make its view prevail at the conference table would cast around for means to make rejection unattractive to its opposite number, and the lack of physical force would simply divert energy into other directions. It can of course be urged that other methods could scarcely be so destructive as modern warfare. Even to this hopeful view there must be two qualifications. The first is that were the battle to be transferred largely to the minds of men, to propaganda and counter-propaganda, it would be a miracle if any sort of freedom of thought survived. The other is a version of our earlier contention—that the abolition of weapons does not mean that they cannot be procured again if necessary. A nation which feels it is losing a vital argument is free, within its resources, to repent in haste of its disarmament. The sum of the matter is that disarmament would not mean the abstraction of the factor of power from international relations, but only the removal of one particular expression of power and the diversion of power to other channels. We are still left with the problem on our hands of how to regulate the relationships of power between nations in some human and rational way, and we will be driven to search in later chapters for means of doing this in terms of supranational institutions. While, of course, disarmament has a very high, if not a primary, place in this sense. Any advance in disarmament both registers and facilitates more relaxed relations between the parties involved. It is thus a touchstone and a catalyst of international goodwill. But the goodwill depends ultimately far more on the assurance that mankind has sufficiently mastered the power of the nation-state, so as to bring it under the control of some system of acceptable international law, which is accompanied by adequate power of enforcement against all comers. Not a reversion to powerlessness but a proper recognition of the realities of power and a firm determination to establish humane control over them is the direction in which 'progress' lies.

In our search for a definition of 'progressive' as a description of the kind of domestic government most likely to co-operate in the tasks of peace, and least easily to be tempted or betrayed into military adventures, we have elaborated two aspects. In view of the revolutionary changes occurring in human societies under the impact of modern science and technology, government must show a degree of flexibility and responsiveness. And this has certain implications about the means whereby pressure for change can be effectively exercised on the supreme political authority of the nation. Secondly, there is the universal demand that government be seen to be a servant of man and not *vice versa*: (what we have called the modern triumph of Bentham). This should not be understood as requiring a reduction in the power of government. Rather it should be seen as a challenge to devise power-systems capable of regulating a world packed full of power of one kind and another, so that these forces become not the mindless and destructive autonomous robots of our night-mares, but are made to serve humane interests. If these two aspects are contemplated together, the composition suggests an unending task as new elements of power arise and in turn demand new efforts of regulation. The two men, Hegel and Marx, who first recognised something of what the industrial revolution might portend for human destiny, and who were stimulated thereby to propound a coherent and exhaustive philosophy of history, both perceived something of what the emerging power-structures would do to human society. Just as delicate sensibilities can be offended by the revelations of Freud, the gritty realism of Marx's understanding of how power could work in society to the destruction of men startles and offends all those who wish to preserve a sentimental and idealistic picture of the human condition. But we are still indebted to these great men for some at least of their suggestions as to what we are and what is happening to us. Hegel and Marx recognised that the dawn of technology marked a decisive change in the human condition. But neither fully appreciated that this was the start of a process of change which has no discernible limit. Both therefore thought of the new situation as essentially transitional between the relatively static world of the feudal age, and the new order which each defined in his own way. For Hegel the picture was of the universal state (a fact to be pondered by all those who hasten enthusiastically towards world government) where men would find their fulfilment in pursuit of those 'great objects, great aims, great contents' of public life. For Marx the situation involved the withering away of the state, and the emergence of an order in which 'with society regulating general production and by this means enabling me to do this today and that tomorrow, to hunt in the morning, fish in the afternoon, carry on animal husbandry in the evening ... ' the private sector of our lives would alone have prominence. In passing it is worth noting the elements of agreement between the vision of Marx in 1846 and the predictions of the cyberneticists of 1966. Yet both Hegel and Marx were reactionaries in the terms we have been using. Both belonged sufficiently to the old static order to imagine that change itself would prove a phase and not a permanent condition. In addition, Marx, for all his recognition of the power factors in the emerging industrial world, associated them falsely with the particular nature of nineteenth century capitalism, and overlooked the fact that they belonged inescapably with the structure of modern industry itself, however it was organised. Both were utopians—and utopianism, far from being progressive, is more often harking back to the dream of a past golden age.

But even if Marx falsely imagined a time when the factor of power in human affairs would 'wither away', he had the perception to recognise the role it would play in the interim—was, indeed, already playing in the emerging society of England of the Industrial Revolution. It is this recognition which represents his lasting contribution to our understanding of our condition. It is no mere superficial parallel that is drawn with the work of Freud—who invaded another area of human experience and made men recognise a reality which they tended to obscure because of its potential threat to their security and self-respect. It marked an important advance in human consciousness when men no longer were content to say 'sex tends to corrupt, and absolute preoccupation with sex corrupts absolutely'. Recognising in some degree the anarchic element in sexuality and its obsessive propensities, yet we can now understand and accept and therefore control this part of our nature better in so far as it has become a matter for serious consideration rather than guilty rejection. Likewise the emphasis Marx placed on the existence of power groups and *foci* in modern society shocked and still shocks those who want a simpler and more innocent picture of the world. But also it puts into more courageous human hands some of the means for controlling the very thing which we feel threatens our humanity.

There is a peculiar version of this suspicion of power to be found in many parts of the intellectual tradition of mankind. For while, in reactionary societies, an intellectual group will learn from Marx to isolate and identify the malevolent power-factors in the situation, once the work of construction begins a traditional reflex begins to take over, and the intellectual tends to withdraw from the engines of power. Lord Acton is then quoted with uncritical reiteration to the effect that power tends to corrupt. 'The notion that political practice inescapably involved moral compromise goes back to Plato, pervades Western philosophy and Western common sense, and has become part of the heritage of intellectuals in most countries of the world. In the West, it is reinforced by traditional suspicions of worldly pomp and power inherited from Prophetic and Christian teachings. In many other civilisations, it is reinforced by religious and philosophical ideas that condemn the world as the scene of illusion and temptation.... The obvious fact should perhaps also be mentioned that the objective experience of most human beings in relation to the wielders of political power has been a bitter one.'[2]

Understandable as this attitude is, at a time when power is escalating in the world, it has become an anachronism—except for those who seek a new monasticism. Granted all the menaces which accompany the modern capacity to organise, control, and

[2] Charles Frankel, US Assistant Secretary of State, in *Foreign Affairs*, October 1965, p. 9.

master more and more of our common experience—if we turn our eyes away they will not disappear. Consequently the aspect of this intellectual tradition which has been picked up and made part of the governing thought of the Protestant churches, and which looks for a future in which power in human affairs no longer menaces, is out of touch with the times. And the recent tendency of Roman Catholic thought on international affairs (struggling to free itself from mediaeval categories) to toy with similar delusions, ought perhaps to be explained on the grounds that the discussion is still at a comparatively early stage.

'Progressive' in such a context, then, and in terms of the task of creating international order, is taken to mean the organising of power itself in such a way that it does not run amok among the nations. It is an idea that leads at once in the direction of the establishment of international structures of law and order, the theme of Chapter VII. But in so far as it is a point of view which recognises the unending nature of the processes of change on which we are embarked, and the challenge ever and anew to create fresh instruments for handling what is novel and original, the modern progressive has come to see that in political terms 'here on earth we have no continuing city'. To what then do we progress? It is perhaps at this point that we should turn again appropriately to the Christian tradition in search of an answer.

6

THE REALISTIC HOPE

IN CHAPTER III we noted how the prophetic tradition of Judaism introduced into human thinking the powerful idea that history had meaning, was moving to a *dénouement*, and, whatever the cost might be in the frustration of false human ambitions, that *dénouement* was essentially to be conceived in terms of promise rather than menace. The explosive effect of this idea fits the revolutionary age in which we now live. Just how far the modern world springs from this conviction born of the Jewish people is a matter for historians to determine, but it is certainly one of the factors which set off the Western world, Christian, humanist or Marxist, upon that rampage of activity which has made it both a promise and a menace to the rest of mankind. Over against the fatalism or the cyclical concept of the historical process, which dominates so much of the rest of the ancient and modern world, here is a principle of purposeful human activity which today for the first time is beginning to capture the imagination of men from one end of the world to the other. In this sense we have entered, as a race, the age of progress.

But we must also note another less generally recognised but equally powerful idea which comes right out of the ancient Jewish world. This is a fundamentally positive evaluation of the material world. In contrast to the great weight of religious tradition (which has found in the physical the manifestation of a decaying yet corrupting and also fascinating prison for the spirit) the Jewish faith asserted that the world was made by God and God found it very good. So did God's people—and their fellows can still be offended by the world-affirming expressions in Jewish culture. Yet here again was the seminal idea which lies at the root of so much scientific adventure, and of that materialism which insists absolutely rightly that we take the physical world and the realities of our life on earth with absolute seriousness. Here is the correction to that notion of religion which makes of it some sort of escape from the human condition and seeks in mystical and esoteric experience an assurance of deeper realities.

'The Marxist Ernst Bloch scolds Christians for having introduced the "principle of hope" into the world, as a category for understanding history, and then having allowed it to be taken from them. He believes that the principle of hope became too dangerous for a church increasingly oriented to the *status quo*. But since such a powerful idea, once it is introduced into history, cannot be banished, it eventually emigrated into radical political and social movements. Christian eschatology was reduced to a personal life after death or the transformation of this world at some final end-of-history return of Christ. In the meantime, any visible hope for historical man was lost.' In this summary Harvey Cox presents very precisely the problem which confronts us in this chapter.[1] If Ernst Bloch is correct, then Christians have betrayed their origins in two respects. Such hope as they have permitted themselves has become detached alike from the historical process and the material world.

But is it not too slick to ascribe this apparent apostasy simply to the economic and class interests of church leaders? Such a simple dramatisation of the past is agreeable to modern mythologists but at least in this case there were obviously other elements at work. For however Christians tried to articulate their hope for history, they had to take account, at the very centre of their experience, of the fact of the death of their Lord at history's hands. So much of his remembered teaching had been in preparation for this event, so central had his death and resurrection been as crucial events declaring the very meaning of his ministry, that somehow all definitions of Christian hope must start from this key point.

We have seen that the significance Jesus Christ himself gave to his ministry, in the records we possess, was less that of an ethical

---

[1] See the article by Harvey Cox in *The Correspondent*, Winter 1965, entitled 'Marxist Humanism in Eastern Europe—Problems and Prospects' (Council for Correspondence, Harvard University, Cambridge, Mass.), p. 40.

originator. Essentially he saw it as the manifestation of the fundamental personal relationship, of love or hostility, in which men stand with the ultimate reality of their lives. He came to announce that, with his arrival, that relationship had reached a new and ultimate phase—not in the future, but now. 'The kingdom is at hand' is to be understood as proclaiming that the long expected day of Jewish hope had arrived. And he went on to preach, and then to show forth in his own flesh and blood, that this relationship cannot be destroyed by the worst that history can do. It is beyond history in the sense that while the material of that relationship is the stuff of our ordinary life (the decisions we make and the way we react to the challenges of every day), yet like all truly personal relations it is not simply a function of these experiences, but possesses a reality of its own. At the same time that reality is not separable from historical experience, and it involves some very mundane and materialistic activity such as giving thirsty people water, or visiting those in jail. Indeed the chosen symbols of that relationship are the most ordinary of ordinary things (at least in Eastern Mediterranean terms), bread and wine. But however ordinary, they are the expressions of a relationship which physical death did not end, but sealed ... 'died for you'.

It is obvious that this central Christian experience could easily tend to cause men to down-grade the significance of historical hope, quite apart from whether or not they were driven by class and economic interests. In fact it appears to have done just this among the earliest of the followers of Jesus Christ who, in Marxist terms, had little to hope from the *status quo*. The first reaction of the Jerusalem congregation was to assume that to all intents and purposes history had come to an end. They anticipated an early consummation, and meanwhile many of them sold all their possessions to give to the poor while they awaited the end—a misunderstanding which gave rise to the first great undertaking of inter-church aid under the guidance of St Paul and others. Others had a different preoccupation—the sense that what they had just experienced was of universal significance, so that they had an urgent obligation to broadcast the news of it as widely as possible. The astonishing, spontaneous missionary enterprise, which we now know was by no means confined to St

Paul and his team, spread rapidly not only through the Middle East and the Roman Empire but may even in the first generation have got to the shores of southern India. This too could be the clue to the meaning of history, men might surmise, that it would be prolonged till the message had got to the ends of the world. All these ideas were going through the mind of the man to whom Christians were turning for theological guidance, St Paul. But of one thing he was clear—those were right who perceived that in Jesus Christ the end of history had been disclosed. Here was the fundamental reality to whom men must be related, and with them, the whole panoply of the created world. Whatever was still to be disclosed about the unfolding of the human story, the whole drama—not only on one planet but of the cosmos in its entirety—would find its meaning in the end in the one who had appeared in Galilee. And only in that relationship, accepted and obeyed, was there real life (Ephesians 1. 3-14; Colossians 1. 12-23).

It has to be said that for centuries Christian thinkers laid aside the problem of defining a Christian understanding of history. No doubt the collapse of the Roman Empire created conditions in which historical optimism was at a discount. No doubt in the immense task of re-creating for the human inhabitants some sort of European order, church and state, Pope and Emperor, were so closely interwoven that the vested interests in the *status quo*, to which Ernst Bloch draws attention, played a part in damping down 'progressive' imagination. It must also be remembered that at a most formative period the Christian community had passed through a series of bitter persecutions which exposed them to an element in the historic process they could not ignore. Indeed they interpreted it firmly in terms of the crucifixion of Jesus Christ. It was the discovery of a basic recalcitrance in the human community, which was capable of bitter resistance to the presentation of the fact of Jesus Christ. Let it not be thought that the qualifications which Christian thinkers insist on placing on all over-enthusiastic human optimism derived solely either from their vested interests or their morbid imaginations. They sprang properly from their own reflection on the sight of our Lord being crucified, and the subsequent experience, in Roman arenas and Greek market places, of the place of martyrdom in Christian life.

The attempt to understand the nature of that recalcitrance has led far beyond the familiar list of human delinquencies. It is not simply that we are, as a race, given to exorbitant fears, intolerances, selfishness, or even the lust, greed and oppression which are often thought to describe the content of the word 'sin'. The basic fault to which Christian thinkers have ascribed all else is that alienation from the source of our being and life, expressed by our determination to set our own goals for ourselves and to be free from the interference of one who claims to be our goal and life. It is not too difficult to see how such a demand of the autonomous will necessarily involve disharmony within the race itself in so far as men will not agree on the definition of the goal. Indeed in the very pursuit of autonomy we will quite deliberately attempt to establish bigger and better goals than the next man in order to justify our demand to be his master, not his slave. We are speaking here of a feature which finds frequent and familiar articulation in international conflicts.

From the Renaissance onwards, however, and at an increasing pressure, Christian thinkers have felt the need to understand afresh the hopes of history. They have had to take into account the realities of the past, but also the emerging world, exciting and stimulating of human mastery. And in the modern ecumenical debate they must reconcile the strain of historical pessimism (a feature of the tradition in those churches stemming from the Roman branch and taking the fact of the crucifixion as a key to our condition) with the greater optimism of the Byzantine theology, which gives pre-eminence to Easter and the prospect of a transfiguration of the world of matter and history. The original and awaited contribution from the developing world of Africa and the ancient cultures of Asia has still to find its indigenous expression. But in the present state of the discussion there is no other way of stating the Christian understanding than that of paradox, reflecting the dualities noted above.

This 'yes and no' to the world and its historical process has been described thus by Bonhoeffer: 'It is the "yes" to what is created, to becoming and to growth, to the flower and to the fruit, to health, happiness, ability, achievement, worth, success, greatness and honour; in short it is the "yes" to the development of the power of life.' Let us examine this more fully before attending to the other side of the paradox. For it is this affirmative which is missing from much popular Christian piety. There is a strangely persistent thread of mystical escapism which Christian churches share with other types of oriental religion—and which is frankly heretical in Christian terms. It shrinks from the acceptance of the physical world, its reality and significance, just because of itself it is not enough, nor is it trustworthy. But in Christian terms the physical world is never seen by itself, only as the visible expression of the activity of a good Creator. It is this which pronounces affirmatively on human life and its history, which gives positive significance to the process from facelessness to individuality, from the instinctive to the self-conscious, from being the plaything of nature to being its master, from empire to self-determination, from the childhood of the human race to its growing maturity. This is the authentication of all the humanists' enterprises to enlarge human potentialities through education, better health, wider human opportunities. This is the sense in which we can recognise and work for 'progress', and learn to discriminate what are the positive elements in that rag-bag of developments which go by the one name of progress, and which all too often we are invited to accept in a single package deal.

The 'no' is derived from the recognition that the whole exciting development of human history as we know it in secular terms does not support the hope which men want to build upon it. The process, so filled with increasing potentiality, is not self-fulfilling and indeed contains a fatal flaw in so far as it proceeds in alienation from that ultimate and supreme relationship which is the source of our life. To take the whole self-absorbed activity of human history and submit it completely to the judgement of him who is its origin and goal is something which feels like death because it involves an unconditional surrender, even of our hopes. So Bonhoeffer can say: 'it is the "no" to that defection from the origin, essence and goal of life inherent in all this existence from the outset. This "no" means dying, suffering, poverty, renunciation, resignation, humility, degradation, self-denial ...'[2] Yet even this negation has about it the note of final affirma-

---

[2] *Ethics*, p. 190. The words are read with reverence as coming from the pen of a man who did what is here described and, affirming life and becoming deeply involved in its affairs, accepted death at the hands of the Nazis as part of the same affirmation.

tion, for it is in such submission that at last we can say 'yes' and have 'yes' said to us in terms which sweep up together the life and beauty of this world and all that is beyond it, in a forgiveness on the other side of the submission of mortality.

Strictly speaking we can discern three modes rather than two in the Christian evaluation of historical hope. The first and third are essentially positive though in different forms, and the second is that which at once offends and disturbs our confidence that we have in our hands the meaning of human existence. The three must be examined in order.

The first is an unashamed affirmation of the value of life, and of its manifestation in all the conditions of this visible world. This unashamed affirmation has to defend itself all the time from the tendency of the religious mind to use religion to escape the limitations and frustrations of actual experience by giving a certain primacy to the products of our imaginations, dreams and longings. The assertion of the Christian tradition is that reality is to be discerned, not in some kind of other world which has to be set over against the one against which we stub our toes every working day, but in a deeper and fuller understanding of the world of our physical and historical experience. The starting point of Christian thought is that we are assured that we are dealing with fundamental reality when we handle, or are handled by, the material historical processes of our lives on this earth. And moreover the reality we thus encounter is good, at the least in the sense that it is not alien to our human nature but is susceptible of understanding and investigation by our minds. Even more than that, the assertion of 'good' has in it the sense that, in spite of the apparent fragility of human life itself, its extreme vulnerability to physical and historical disaster, there is an ultimate sense in which we can believe that the world is trustworthy, and human enterprise and adventure in it is worthwhile.

The way we thus echo the phrase of Bonhoeffer, that the Christian faith says 'yes' to the development of the power of life, has particular reference to the process we examined in the previous chapter—whereby human power, and its organisation into great *foci* of power, becomes an inescapable and accelerating feature of our contemporary history. The prospect may well appear daunting to the classical humanist, and the instincts of men may cause them to shrink away from such a destiny of history. Then religion will be called in to utter nostalgic remonstrances about the direction in which events seem to be taking us all: away from the simpler, more 'human', more innocent because more impotent, world of the past. It is at that point that the test comes, whether we truly believe the Christian affirmation about the development of the power of life—whether in the last analysis we believe in life itself, and, in these terms, in a meaningful progress of history. The progress we must then assert, and to which we ought eagerly to commit ourselves, concerns that enlargement of our understanding of ourselves and our environment (and with it the power it puts in our hands to control and determine nature and history together) which has become a real promise to our race in modern times. Nor will this challenge come simply in abstract or philosophical terms. It presents itself, for instance, in the way we appreciate the human cry for 'self-determination'. Of course we can derive from Christian understanding no specific policies or timetables with which powerful states should respond to this demand. But we can align ourselves with those who claim that the destiny of history requires men, without distinction but simply as men, to be accorded the right to devise their own responses to the questions put to them by life itself. And if the great and growing concentrations of power in the world, left to themselves, would tend rather to increase the dominance of those already powerful, this does not mean that the development of power is in itself inherently wrong. Rather it points to the inadequacy of the devices we have evolved to direct and control it. Power should be seen not as a menace to 'self-determination' but an instrument on which self-determination can be exercised to the greatest extent possible.

But the second mode of Christian understanding must equally be taken into account, organically related to the first, yet bearing its negative and tragic corrective. It is not, as some traditional religions and philosophies have asserted, that our woes stem from our imprisonment in the physical world or simply our inescapable participation in the long guilt of history. Nor is it that we are still in the process of evolving a moral discipline to match our greater powers. (It is hard to make a sensible case, for instance, for the contention that we show a more markedly moral sensitivity than, let us say, the psalmists of three thousand years ago.) The issue is seen as far more fundamental, involving a basic fault in the human relation with reality itself. Whereas it is 'natural' for men to consider themselves as autonomous, using and disposing of the inanimate world, and even each other, in accordance with a 'self-determined' judgement of what they think is good, it is a fundamentally disturbing challenge to acknowledge that our basic relationship is personal, and involves coming to terms with a will which is not our will, which appears at first as a strange and possibly threatening will, whose demands upon us cut across our own chosen destiny. But if this be the case, then the progress of mankind from man's narrow confinement in the necessities of nature to his growing and self-conscious dominance over nature, is a progress which carries within it no necessary promise of peace. Rather it opens the prospect of greatly enlarged capacities for pursuing alike both good and ill.

Does this make us withdraw or qualify what we have already asserted positively? The answer is not lightly to be given by anyone who has begun to understand the element of threat to the race which modern scientific discovery contains, and which is represented, but not exhausted, by the menace of nuclear war. Or again, the spectacle of masses of hungry, exploited or despised members of our human family—does it not portend a peaceless future in which the experience of war may be even more universal than anything known to date? Would it not be better, after all, at least to try to reduce the speed of the whole development? Once we have had the courage to dispense with the easy optimism of those who turn their eyes away from the tragic element in history, these are the real questions to be answered. They receive attention in the third mode of the Christian understanding of historical hope.

But we must first elaborate a little more the way in which the tragic element of history, as Christians understand it, expresses itself. At the most superficial level, it is represented by the whole problem which politics arises to resolve our inability to discern and agree upon common goals for our living activity. Autonomy raises the problem of co-operation. We want conflicting things. But even more, we demand the right to priority for our views in the matter, or else we are enslaved to another human will. As we shall see in a later chapter, the whole apparatus of ideological controversy grows from this seed—partly a kind of loyalty to our own conception of the good, partly a rationalisation of our demand that *we* should be the arbiter of what is good. Within the confines of human history as we know it empirically we thus see the issue of our radical disharmony. It is an act of faith (with rational justification much less cogent than the Christian faith supplies) to believe that there is some simple or accessible way in which we shall be able to overcome this problem of the assertive human will.

There is a deeper sense still, however, in which this tragic insight qualifies our idea of progress. Taken at its ordinary level, the idea of progress suggests that we know what the goal is and that we can therefore measure degrees of proximity. We have already seen reason to accept a version of the idea of progress which takes the enlargement of human capacity and self-consciousness as its objective. But without subtracting anything from that, we must now add that this remains only a partial answer. For what end and purpose is man to occupy these enlarged capacities? They are, after all, capacities, potentialities only, which in the end must be assessed by the use to which they are put. And our problem is not only that we cannot agree with one another what those uses should be, but, in Christian understanding, we are fatally deceived about the very nature of the good itself. If it is fulfilment, life, enlargement, power, it is also submission to the perfect will, which involves equally suffering, renunciation and, as the most typical symbol, dying. Whatever our definition of Christian hope in historical terms, a place has to be found for what has been traditionally called 'judgement'—the process of extrication of the real from the imaginary, of God's good from what we have accepted as good, for the purgatorial experience of having our bounding adventure of living judged but not destroyed. The terms traditionally used to carry this meaning have been 'death' and 'resurrection'. The problem for Christian thinking is to give content to these terms in relation to the historical process itself. The inherited myths speak of a last day, a day of judgement at once asserting the ultimacy of life and destroying the pretensions and falsities of life in isolation from its source. The imagery combines the figure of death in the form of destroying fires, and the figure of true fulfilment of life in the form of the 'rising' of all just men, of a new heaven and a new earth. If this mediaeval imagery no longer has meaning for our modern minds, we are still nevertheless obliged to express in a more adequate way the sense in which Christians qualify and limit the concept of secular historical hope. While the myths[3] themselves elude us, we can at least delineate in the form outlined what it is they will have to convey. They must express in the first place the faith that cosmic decay and physical death are not of themselves the total account of the end of human history. The basic assertion that has to be made is not of endless continuance, but of fulfilment as the final verdict of the human story. But the fulfilment must not be so represented that it amounts to depicting an ultimate generation of humans rejoicing because they stand above the wreck and frustration of all their forefathers' existence. It must be a representation which gives significance to what we are all doing now—a present rather than merely prospective evaluation. And it must take account of the reality both of progress and of judgement, which discriminates in historical development between good and evil, and prevents us asserting that because certain developments which are new take place, they must be good because they represent 'progress'. Above all the myth we need has to indicate that central personal relationship which supplies the ultimate meaning to history, and of which history is the record of our human rejection and recognition. And it has to affirm that the last word lies with the God whom we reject.

Does this not empty of any sort of exciting content all those

[3] I have used the word 'myth' in a rather technical sense, and not in its *Oxford English Dictionary* definition of 'a purely fictitious narrative usually involving supernatural persons'. The sense in which I have used it is that of a pictorial presentation of a truth which, lying outside our present experience, can only be presented to the imagination in this form.

hopes which stir us to selfless action and noble purpose? If we cannot wholeheartedly believe that the long historical process is relentlessly leading forward to brighter and better things, to peace and prosperity, does it not cut the nerve of that dynamic, satisfying, and costly effort to ameliorate the human condition which we instinctively feel the times demand? If, for instance, it is true that the kind of progress in which we are involved carries with it the chance to build more self-consciously stable and just international order, such progress also has features which make that objective even harder to attain. The awakening human race, argumentative and capable at last of articulating its very different aspirations, is much harder to organise than might have been a pact of self-interest between a couple of satisfied emperors. And if at the same time, with the advent of nuclear weapons, the collapse of international order holds unimaginable threats to the race, is it possible to engender any real enthusiasm (informed by realistic analysis) for the purpose of putting an end to war? How does one live creatively in so ambiguous a historical process? This is the question which has to be answered in the third of the modes we have foreseen, in terms which are essentially positive.

In this aspect of the matter the emphasis is on the present, rather than the future. Here Christian thinking begins from the affirmation: 'He is risen'. The faith we assert is that the basic personal relation in which our lives are set is a present reality, and a reality which has survived historical disaster, or more accurately has overcome such disaster. The 'end' has already appeared, and even in this ambiguous historical existence it is demanded of us that we live in that relation. It means further that to live faithfully and confidently in that relation involves seeking to achieve its expression—peace, forgiveness, love and life—in the affairs of men: as far as that is possible, given the nature of the material with which we are working. Beyond this again, it involves the readiness to bear witness to a more perfect order than we can ever achieve in history of ourselves—even at the cost of historical failure, if thereby men can catch a better glimpse of their real destiny.

In trying to follow this obedience all the acute problems arise which can so readily lead to fruitless controversy, so long as protagonists attempt to establish their own convictions as the only right ones. How much of the task of peace-making, for instance, requires a sober and realistic acceptance of the way men and societies do in fact respond, as revealed by the studies of social scientists, psychologists, political scientists, historians—and indeed men of compassion all through the ages? How much of the testimony to another mode of life is lost if too readily we appear to accept the habits of our normal existence? At what point are we obliged, for the sake of men and their future on earth, to get down to the rough job of rigging up structures for immediate use with what gear we have, rather than calling attention to a way of life that is not available in our present human condition? But how then do we give expression to another mode of existence, on the far side of our alienation from the ground and source of our life? There are no simple answers, and the dialogue between pacifist and non-pacifist within the Christian community represents the fact that this is so. It is only when one or other party to the dialogue presumes to try to conclude it in his favour that damage is done to the integrity of Christian truth. For the ambiguity with which we wrestle is simply a reflection of the situation in which our lives are set, the being and the becoming both together of our life on earth.

At the end of the argument we must now re-estimate what contribution, in the light of the understanding of Christian faith, 'progressive' political forces make to the establishment of peace. In the terms in which we have understood 'progress,' we have to say that in certain important respects the evolution of mankind to a more self-conscious, powerful, individualistic existence greatly complicates the problem of achieving a workable harmony on a universal scale. The easy utopianism, which often accompanies an uncritical adoption of a 'progressive' point of view, is a dangerous temptation to turn away from the reality of the problem—on the bland assumption that it does not exist, or if it does exist that it will yield its own solution as progress proceeds. On the other hand, the process of human awakening provides us with new tools of understanding which we can use if we will to make the problem manageable. Moreover it presents us also with a threat of such dimensions as to compel a certain attention and priority to the creation of the conditions for international peace. We have to guard against a superficial optimism that comes easily to those most keenly aware of the newness of the day on which mankind is entering, and which shrinks from spoiling the wonder of its own dream by attending to the possibility of its turning into a nightmare. But equally it is of the essence of Christian conviction to insist that there is complete validity in working now, realistically and tirelessly, to realise as far as possible within history the reality which is not confined in history. Moreover, such activity is freed from the sense of futility or despair which comes from hope long deferred or the failure of our efforts—in so far, that is, as it draws its justification from a relationship which the disaster of crucifixion has not annulled, but rather given indestructible meaning in the light of the Easter resurrection.

Such realistic activity for peace will wrestle with the new constellations of power, their manipulation in the modern world, and the political devices which must be developed if men are to find instruments other than war for dealing with their conflicts. This leads straight into the third major theme of this book—the contribution of international structures to the establishment of peace.

7

INSTITUTIONS OF PEACE

'To ENSURE PEACE, it is not enough to praise its benefits, or even to agree to keep it. War must be prevented by suitable institutions'. This aphorism of the fourteenth century (already quoted) defines the subject for this chapter. We have to sketch first the nature of the necessity referred to, and then to consider the positive and negative factors working for this kind of development in our contemporary world. Then we must ask, in terms of the human condition as we have examined it earlier in this book, how much reliance we can properly place on this proposal to achieve the condition of relatively stable peace. Can we identify those aspects of our affairs which must first be attended to before effective institutions can be established on a universal scale?

It is possible to make a theoretical scheme representing three stages in the evolution of our attempts to resolve the problems of the conflict of large human groups, a scheme which does not depart too far from historical experience. The most primitive stage is that in which the confrontation of one group or tribe by another, rivals for land or food or authority, is one of hostility to be worked out simply according to the arbitrament of physical force. No other relationship between the two groups is attempted other than the dominance of one by the other, or its withdrawal from the scene. It is to this stage we revert when we desperately submit our modern conflicts to military solutions, although we have at least learned that the end product can be the entry to stage two. This second stage is reached when the two sides accept the possibility of parleying, and are prepared, either before or after displaying their panoply of arms, to see whether the par-

ticular conflict cannot be abated sufficiently for practical purposes by negotiating for a compromise solution. Already at this
stage 'suitable institutions' enter the picture. For evidently it is in
practice much easier to get men and nations to pass from stage
one to stage two if there already exist the facilities which are
needed for working out together some sort of acceptable bargain
—the means to bring the parties physically into each other's
presence, the lines of communication which allow soundings to
be taken discreetly beforehand, even so ordinary a requirement
as a locality for meeting which renders neither side personally
insecure, and does not of itself imply an initial concession. When
we try to assess the utility of the United Nations we should not
neglect this very practical aspect of the matter, nor allow it to be
swamped by more extravagant pretensions. One of the main
reasons for believing that if the United Nations were destroyed
we should have to begin immediately inventing a new one is that
we simply cannot get on any longer without the basic facilities
for personal meeting, the relatively 'uncommitted' *milieu*, the
opportunity on a permanent basis of carrying on international
political conversation which the UN provides. If the conversation often is vastly unreal or wearisomely prolonged this is the
price we require our diplomats to pay for keeping available all
the apparatus needed in moments of tension and crisis, when the
conversation very quickly becomes a great deal more real,
though correspondingly inaudible to the world outside.

The third stage is reached when men pass from providing
themselves with the means for talking out a conflict between
themselves, and enter into arrangements of a general kind,
meant to cover future conflicts as they arise, so that the terms of
their resolution are already agreed and foreseen in some degree.
This is the stage at which men set up 'laws', broad statements of
principle or specific regulations intended to apply over a wide
range of eventualities. When men pass from the stage of *ad hoc*
negotiation of conflict as it arises to the stage of legality they
have evidently crossed a critical boundary in terms of recognising the permanency of their community with one another. This
accounts for the almost transcendent significance given to 'the
rule of law' in human societies. Men have found here a defence
against arbitrary power: an instrument for advancing from

oligarchies and tyrannies to communities in which men are in some recognisable degree treated seriously, regardless of the power they can personally deploy to defend their own interests. The ideal of such societies is that conflicts have to be submitted, not to the determination of who is the stronger, not to the horse-trading of *ad hoc* negotiations, but to the adjudication of an impartial tribunal or court required to judge according to laws generally accepted as fair in the cool rationality before conflict has arisen.

Evidently this third stage is the one which represents the crux of our international problem. How far can we establish all the institutions which belong to it? The extent of the question is even greater than yet appears For in societies which arrange their domestic affairs according to the rule of law, there are great areas and issues of the highest consequence which are handled by political rather than juridical apparatus. What a nation is to do with its wealth, its economy, its political or military power; how it is to adjust the claims and responsibilities of the individual citizen and the community; what balance it can or should strike between the various social forces within the one society—all these crucial questions are left to be determined in the dynamic, changing, contending activity of its political institutions. If law represents the factor of stability and fundamental security in a society, then politics is the arena of growth and development, to the extent even of framing new law. The observation is of particular significance in relation to international affairs, where, in so far as we can foresee in this century, the factor of change is likely far to exceed in importance and difficulty anything which could be legally established as permanent and stable. We shall have to give this consideration full weight when we determine what we are principally seeking in the form of international institutions—instruments of an international rule of law, or apparatus for achieving acceptable international political decisions; the framework of order, or the means of achieving agreed methods of change?

Meanwhile, we can see that the direction of the three-stage evolution sketched above is away from seeking solutions by the application of raw force, and towards as much rationality and consent as possible. Let us not, however, disguise the fact that the rule of law and the compromises of politics are themselves made ultimately effective by those other devices which put physical power at the disposal of the courts of law and the government. Such urbanities as the learned judges can command, such tributes as a government may constantly pay to its dependence on the popular will—all these are elegant proprieties which conceal the fact that these authorities do not in the end simply express opinions, but utter commands and possess the means of making them effective. This represents both their promise and their threat: a promise to those who entrust some of their self-determination into their hands that they will not be left at the mercy of other stronger elements in society; a threat to all individuals who find themselves at odds with the general will. But clearly the development from force to law and politics requires that the ultimate sanction of force in the latter should remain as far as possible latent, and should where necessary exist in such preponderance that it is never overtly and seriously challenged. This in turn has implications both for law and for politics. The law to be enforced must be such as generally is acceptable to the minds and consciences of the people, or perhaps more cautiously, does not seriously offend their sense of what is right and fair. To this extent it cannot be something externally imposed but must to an important degree grow out of, and be rooted in, the general cultural values and moral convictions of the society. If a law has to be imposed against the wishes of a significant number of the citizens it has ceased to do its proper job, which is to maximise the elements of rationality and consent in comparison with the exercise of sheer power. The point to be noted here is that international law, in the sense of the elaboration of a whole system on which world order could be stabilised, depends not simply on the willingness of sovereign states to submit their conflicts to international jurisdiction, but more fundamentally on the gradual formation in humanity at large of sufficient common conviction to sustain and accept a system of common law. That a beginning can and should be made where possible is certain; there are technical and administrative questions which lend themselves to this kind of treatment already. We might hope, for instance, to see the law of the sea elaborated by common consent without delay. But the procedures for agreeing anything like a universal system of human rights legislation are likely to prove monotonously protracted just because the issues at stake are of such great human consequence, and the minds of men are at such great variance about them. There is no short cut, by designing better theoretical codes of law, more ingenious judicial systems, or apparent inducements to states to submit themselves to the legal processes thus evolved, which avoids the problem of securing something of a common mind to start with.

The same applies to the political system. Whatever means we invent to make possible the transfer of political power from one group to another in accordance with some method of expressing the popular desire, the whole machinery will work as an alternative to the crude exercise of power only if it operates within a broad framework of general agreement. Variables are susceptible to determination by majority vote, fundamentals are not; and what men think are variables and what fundamentals is the measure of a society's convictions. The viability of an international political system will therefore depend on the degree to which there already exists a minimum of common conviction about fundamentals within which the system can work.

The absence of such a minimum of common conviction is itself doubted by many people today, who believe that, were we more honest, we would recognise a broad agreed understanding of the meaning of secular humanism. They are a little impatient of the complex dogmatisms of ideologies which appear to them to be invented as much to justify separatism and divisiveness as to give sincere expression to deeply held views. It is very important to examine seriously this criticism of ideologies, religious or political, for it contains a very significant element of truth. But in doing so it would be well to admit from the outset that it is hard to make an ideology do its work if it has no basis in experience. It must represent some element of truth if it is to appeal to a multitude of minds, even if this truth is grossly exaggerated or seriously distorted.

Ideologies[1] perform two functions for us. The first is to give satisfaction to our hope that life has deeper meaning than is

[1] For a stimulating critique of ideologies, Christian, Marxist and liberal-democratic, and a constructive attempt to define some essential humane values, see Patrick Corbett, *Ideologies* (Hutchinson, London, 1965).

supplied simply by the need to survive as long as possible. They therefore represent evidence of the demand of our human nature that we seek a significance in existence beyond that which is inherent in nature itself. There is a constantly recurring example of this which continuously reasserts itself when the rich and powerful nations find themselves in conflict with the poor and weak. It has often been pointed out that a developing nation's addiction to independence is liable to have negative economic consequences for a population already needy enough. The moral is drawn that such nations would be wiser to consult first their economic interests, and never mind the grandeurs of political independence till they can better afford them. It is, objectively, surprising that men will thus think of one another. For if there is one thing on which it is possible to get agreement between human beings it is that there is something unworthy of our race in a readiness to sell one's self-respect for a bowl of soup. And our self-respect demands the right to reach our own definition of the meaning of our own and our nation's history, and not to have to accept such a definition from others. Thus an ideology can manifest itself in terms of a nationalism which articulates a particular character and identity for one's own nation, in comparison with others. This then is the ambience of meaning in which one's own personal life finds its significance. Or an ideology may more familiarly be developed as an exalted form of political philosophy, transcending the narrow boundaries of states, and in principle offering a universal meaning. Thus the modern contenders for world acclaim, giving themselves names which are different from those accorded to them by their rivals—communism in its various forms of Stalinism, Marxist-Leninism, Revisionism (according to which side the spectator stands upon); democracy, Western capitalism, bourgeois liberalism and the rest. All are inflated by one party or the other to the sacrosanct proportions of truths of fundamental consequence for the whole future of mankind. Evidently theology itself has entered this field; and when church and state have been closely interwoven, it has at times produced what amounts to a particular form of political ideology.

There are two deductions which can be drawn from this human habit of seeking ideological definitions. One is that men

find no contentment unless they, or some of them, can understand the life of their communities in history in terms which
accord it a nobility and importance beyond the preoccupations
of the moment. This has not always been so, nor is it true of those
cultures which are rooted in world-denying forms of religion. It
may be, as has already been suggested, that it is a phenomenon
which owes much of its vitality to the tradition born of the
Hebrew prophets of old, and to the further development of this
tradition in certain parts of the Christian tradition. But wherever
it sprang from, it appears to be now an inescapable part of our
modern world, the more indispensable as we find ourselves borne
along in an accelerating process of change which requires
us constantly to attend to the problem of choosing the right
direction. The choice of direction implies some general idea of
where the process itself ought to be leading. For these reasons
we cannot hope that the problem of conflicting ideologies is
one which will prove a temporary feature of this particular
phase.

But the second deduction is that the other man's ideology is
liable to appear as a means which he adopts to gain power over
us. Ideologies do not present themselves as cool contributions to
an academic discussion, but as weapons in the struggle for power.
This is the second function which ideologies perform for men.
For evidently, if the human problem is in one respect the question of how, in a world of rival wills, a person or a group can
proceed with their own purposes, the options for dealing with
recalcitrant other wills are clear. It is possible to eliminate or
overpower them physically, which is war. Or one can bring to
bear less violent pressures and inducements, and strike a bargain
from as strong a position as it is possible to achieve without using
force; thus making minimised concessions to the other in ex-
change for being allowed to proceed with the greater part of
one's own intention. But best of all would be the capacity to
persuade the other will to accept one's own purposes, and to feel
an inner obligation to collaborate. The way to do this is, consciously or unconsciously, offered by the possibility of elaborating an ideology which gives transcendant justification to the
purposes which one welcomes, and passes some form of moral
denunciation on those who resist. By this means the mutual frus-

tration of wills can be overcome in a manner favourable to the man who has selected and advocated an ideology suitable to his interests.

It is scarcely necessary to follow the working out of this process in terms of communism, democracy, anti-colonialism, western civilisation, democratic socialism, secularism or whatever the selected ideology may be. The adverse features are always the same—a highly selective account of historical experience, a constant attempt to force new experience into the required pattern, a posture of political self-righteousness, and a serious difficulty in coming to terms with the contradictory because the whole hidden purpose of the exercise is precisely to eliminate contradiction.[2] But because of the particular nature of this book, it is worth drawing attention to one particular manifestation of this recourse to ideology as a method of exerting power without appearing to do so; and that is the habit of moralising politics. This is the traditional method of those too scrupulous to use the cruder forms of compulsion, whose image of the world (described as 'bourgeois' by their critics) is kindly and comfortable and therefore does not allow for those expressions of self-will which are outwardly offensive to others, but who at the same time are driven by strong compulsions to put right what in their eyes disfigures the bright image of how things should be. The only instrument of action for them is the proclamation of a moral duty to do as they think ought to be done. The Achilles' heel of this position is the immense difficulty such people have in recognising the degree to which the moral system they favour is designed unconsciously to create the least disturbance to themselves and the greatest change of heart in others. Or to put it in

[2] Illustrations abound. To an outsider part of the embarrassment into which the US government got itself over the struggle in Vietnam arose from the attempt to interpret the struggle chiefly in ideological terms—of the conflict between a cruel and tyrannous communism and a humane and freedom-loving democracy. It needed little special knowledge to perceive how difficult it was to square the actual conduct of affairs in Vietnam with such a picture of reality. Yet the ingrained ideological preoccupations of American political thought made it virtually impossible to state in blunt terms that one of the over-riding problems is to stabilise a power line between China and the USA, a necessity which would exist whatever ideology each professed. In a similar fashion we can observe the contortions in the Communist world to try to fit economic, political and human realities into the narrow constrictions of a pretentious ideology.

another way, men once again by this route find a way of giving universal authority to their particular judgements, and strive to create a sense of obligation to act in a certain way without fully recognising their partiality as judges. It can be a peculiarly subtle device for exercising power, the more dangerous because the user is not conscious of what he is doing.

This is not to say that political problems do not involve serious moral ingredients. Depending on our chosen definition of morality, it is broadly true to say that no really significant political choice can be made merely on technical grounds; it involves considerations of such scope as would be bound to be included in most people's concept of morality. The point is that the choice is never simply moral. Those who claim that it is are most suspect of the trick we have been describing—of using moral categories to create a system of universal obligation favourable to their own interests. The signs of such a performance are two-fold. One is that the morality appealed to is one which requires others to make concessions, rather than the side propounding it. The other is that the problem is presented as 'a simple moral issue' whereas in real life moral issues never occur simply but only in perplexing conflict with each other; so that we are not relieved of the responsibility of determining our own judgement of the right balance in a given situation. Anyone presenting a problem in simple moral terms can be reasonably suspected of a more tortuous if half-conscious mental process—of having some cherished political opinions or objectives which in fact govern the choice he makes, and of being prepared to present them for general acceptance done up in moral terms, as a form of sales promotion. It is the implicit search for power over other wills, which goes with this type of moralism, which is offensive to our human conscience, and which leads so often to a negative appraisal of 'do-gooders'.

This discussion of ideologies started with the question whether men had enough common understanding of the nature and direction of human life to support a universal system of law and politics. We recognised that a system of the rule of law, or a political device for resolving social conflicts without overt resort to pressure and force, depended on a substantial element of consent on fundamental issues. That is to say, the rule of law or the establishment of constitutional forms of government are not means of resolving fundamental conflict but signs that a society has already to an important extent done so. If this is not so, the question asked of the law is 'Whose law?'; and in some measure every legal system represents the priorities and interests of those with power in the land. If such people are seriously divorced, in life and interest, from the majority of the population, the rule of law is scarcely distinguishable from a sophisticated and apparently respectable form of tyranny. In terms of international affairs, the poorer and less powerful nations of the world cannot be expected to welcome the development of a system of international law elaborated by the rich and powerful. They will rightly suspect that such a stabilisation is premature and represents a desire to give permanence to a privileged and agreeable position. The gap in interest and experience is too wide to be quickly bridged by mere laws. In the same way, a system of deciding issues of a political nature by majority vote no longer works as an alternative to force if the fundamental cohesion and common view of a society breaks down. Where for instance modern societies today are riven by racial conflict, parliaments worked on the majority principle are not capable of offering a means of resolving the rivalry so long as power is thus transferred on a 'winner takes all' basis. This basis suffices only so long as what the winner takes is not of very great consequence, and the underlying unanimity as to the nature of a society's unity is left untouched.

What are the chances that men will recognise that they have sufficient in common to support a universal political and legal system? There are obviously two prerequisites. One is that they find a pragmatic method of defining the universal common interest which leaves open the ideological debate. The other is that the immense gap of power and economic advantage between the nations should be substantially narrowed. We must look at both these requirements in further detail before answering the question whether a universal system is possible, or, even if it is, whether it is humanly desirable. Then in that context we can make a more practical assessment of the kind of international institutions which are accessible to men at this point of history, as a means of ensuring peace.

The first requirement of a universal system, the discovery of a pragmatic method of defining the universal common interest which leaves open the ideological debate, appears at first sight to subtract from the political scene precisely those moral considerations of justice and righteousness which it should be the concern of the religious mind to defend and preserve. It will be the task of the next chapter to look more closely at this particular side of the problem, and to determine in what sense a true religion is properly concerned to 'demythologize' politics. But keeping within the broad assumptions of this present chapter, without using religious presuppositions directly, it can be seen that so long as ideologies have the ambiguous function already ascribed to them, at once attempting to accord a deeper significance to our common life than the struggle of acquisitiveness and survival, and at the same time providing us with an invaluable weapon for imposing our wills on others, they provide little prospect of human unity. On the one hand their affirmations, by their very nature, will never be final or generally satisfying, but always subject to further experience and insight. And on the other hand the temptation to defend or contradict will always be inextricably interwoven with the desire to sustain or overthrow a particular structure of power associated with the orthodoxy in debate. More fundamentally, there is here a critical question of human freedom. One of the noblest assertions of human liberty which we acknowledge in history is the action of the lonely individual or small group which has challenged the general orthodoxy of the day, and often through suffering and apparent rejection has pioneered a new road of development for our race. A world in which men have come to accept a universal ideology would be one which could well prove wholly suffocating for the human spirit. 'It is bad to be oppressed by a minority, but it is worse to be oppressed by a majority....; from the absolute will of an entire people there is no appeal, no redemption, no refuge but treason'. De Tocqueville could not have contemplated, in these words, a majority which reached to the ends of the earth, but this is what we must contemplate if ever we conceive of the possibility of a universal ideology.

We must therefore ask whether it is conceivable that we can jointly acknowledge some ground rules of human conduct which we can all recognise as valid while remaining, corporately, ideologically agnostic. One direction in which we can hopefully look is towards the simple principle of reciprocity, of formally according to other individuals and groups the rights we think it reasonable to demand for ourselves. And conversely we can abjure those claims for ourselves which we find unreasonable when made by others. Much of our domestic law in fact is built on such simple principles, and the only ideological premise necessary to support them is that mankind possesses a common capacity to reason. It may well be that the apocalyptic threat of modern war will provide us with sufficient stimulus to work out some basic rules of international conduct based on a common desire to survive in history. The attempt to do so should not be inhibited by any fear that it is intrinsically impossible in a world of religious and ideological pluralism. At this level at least the secular humanists are right when they assert that we can go a long way before it is necessary to determine fundamental issues of metaphysics.

But there is one issue where it is much less easy to dodge ultimate questions—the right relation of individuals to the community. Here men almost universally sense a matter of general consequence. And they can readily perceive that it cannot be settled by some rule of thumb reference to reciprocal obligations, because in this case there cannot be any real reciprocity. But this is the issue which tends today to make international conflict verge always in the direction of international civil war, in that violence from without can so often be justified as an attempt to go to the aid of an oppressed group within a nation. All wars nowadays present themselves either as wars of liberation or as defence against the aggression of those who believe they are conducting wars of liberation. All ideologies nowadays are attempts to justify a particular resolution of the conflict between the human claims of persons and the power of corporate institutions. The answer which must be given to this dilemma, in the terms of this chapter, is that there is no final resolution of these tensions —between the demands of human persons in their individual integrity, and the claims and power of corporate institutions—

and that any ideological assertion that the perfect answer is discoverable is pretentious. But just because power lies always, and increasingly, with the corporate organisation, that which demands constant vigilance in its defence is the right of the human person in his individual integrity. These assertions can be sustained along with a high degree of agnosticism in religion or philosophy, so long as there remains respect for human nature as such. In fact, of course, all persuasive ideologies sell themselves by advertising their adherence to 'freedom', and their differences arise in the means they propose to reach that goal. Their complaint against rival ideologies is, not that they offer too many concessions to the human person, but that in practice their offer is fraudulent.

It appears, therefore, that the effort to work out universal definitions of human rights is not necessarily vain or attendant upon some still-to-be-achieved moral consensus. The real battle is confined to no one culture or system. It is the never-ending struggle to see that powerful organised interests in state or society are prevented from over-riding human rights whenever it is in their interests to do so. Definitions are but a beginning, and the machinery of protection, capable of withstanding the challenge of powerful interests, is hard to develop and keep in working order. But one of the chief safeguards of human rights in such a situation of growing inequality of power is the common conviction of the community at large. And this is greatly fortified when the cause it is required to defend is clearly and publicly articulated in the form of generally accepted statements of principle. One of the great tasks before us is therefore the agreement on formulations of human rights, not only at the level of the United Nations but also in the regional organisations of Africa, Latin America and Europe, and wherever else nations meet corporately to develop their common life together.

But all such legislation is little more than a hobby while men have no assurance that, when the test comes, power will not be used in the interests of the sectional groups which possess it, rather than in support of law. We have already noted two serious limitations to the development of international institutions. One is that, in a rapidly changing world, law itself (the record of agreed methods of dealing with conflicts) may be less important than political institutions, capable of handling more flexibly the dynamism of the modern world. The other is the gross imbalance in the distribution of power in the world, so that the kind of law which those with power are likely to be ready to enforce is the kind which does not radically disturb the privileged position of a minority of mankind. And in so far as political institutions are intended to be the market-place where bargains are struck about the nature and direction of change in society, they are not themselves instruments for the major redistribution of power. Rather they are the forum where the existing distribution is taken seriously and recognised—without necessarily much pleasure. For all these reasons, the further evolution of international political and legal systems must depend far more on a fairer distribution of power among the nations, than upon some development of an agreed philosophy.

The existing confrontation of nations is between a minority— a minority with technical and therefore economic, financial, military and human resources which are themselves developing at an accelerating rate—and a majority, not only starting late but with diminishing prospects of ever narrowing the gap. The only kind of power in which the majority excel is that of human numbers. But in this respect, hopefully, they are not unlike those social groups in industrial societies which, in the past century, have found a means of organisation where their numbers have been made to count as real power against those with more visible access to the same commodity in different forms. It has proved, historically, to be a matter of organisation and the development of solidarity which has enabled the poor and weak and numerous effectively to assert their demands upon the few and powerful. No doubt this will also prove to be the case on the international scene. But if it is not to be a vastly explosive and destructive development, it is necessary that there should be a place where the majority can recognise one another, can find facilities for organisation, and can confront the powerful in a context of reason and debate where demands can be pressed and acceded to without resort to the bludgeon. This surely is one of the primary functions of the United Nations in the years ahead: obscured by those who insist on seeing it as a world government in embryo, but valued by all who recognise its worth as a forum and a market-place and think none the worse of it for that. Such a role however would put high on the list of significant UN activities such functions as are now being created in connexion with the UN Conference on Trade and Development—perhaps above what its sponsors had originally conceived to be the UN's chief preoccupation, the task of peace-keeping itself. The latter must inevitably be, under existing circumstances of power, represented by a series of *ad hoc* operations, where the expertise of the UN Secretariat is married to the particular constellation of power and interest involved in each conflict as it arises. This produces something less than a solution, but also, it is profoundly to be hoped, the kind of delaying, retarding, inhibiting influence so urgently necessary in a nuclear world.

The case has often been made for requiring the affluent nations to share their wealth with the rest, on the grounds that otherwise peace itself will be destroyed. The matter can be presented in a crude way which suggests that the problem is to supply hungry mouths lest they turn in desperation and rend you. Thus the emphasis is placed on economic need rather than on inequality of power. This makes it a much easier case to present to the affluent, who have goods to spare, and who can therefore provide for the needy without having to forgo anything. But it obscures the real challenge. For what the 'third world' really demands is not simply a higher living standard, but, far more fundamentally, a say in running the world. It is power which has to be shared, not simply goods. This will prove the real difficulty, but until it takes place no viable international institutions are likely to emerge. It is more than likely that the third world itself does not accurately calculate the size of the thing it is demanding, or the responsibilities attending it. But there is no return now along the path which nations took when they challenged the whole conception of empire.

8

TRUE RELIGION IN THE
POLITICAL REALM

THE PREVIOUS CHAPTER exposed the fact that mankind
appears to face a choice. Either to succumb to a new form of
imperialism—ideological imperialism—whereby a frame of
unity is found for the purpose of achieving peace by the im-
position of one particular orthodoxy about the meaning and
values of human existence. Or to try to make do with a system of
pragmatic reciprocity allied to a tolerant sort of ideological
pluralism. At the same time, it was recognised that men are
simply unable to leave alone the ultimate questions of meaning
in life and history, and however perversely they use their arguments to assert their own wills over others, they are nevertheless
talking about something of total consequence to mankind. Is
there any significance in human life and striving other than
what can be crudely found in the rest of nature? For this reason
any system of pragmatic reciprocity with ideological pluralism is
bound to be provisional and essentially unstable. It commends
itself most persuasively in the historical aftermath of great ideological wars, when for a time men are ready to accord priority to
peace above the struggle to realise meaning. We may be approaching the end of one such phase. But once the weariness and
exhaustion have been mended, the race will once again bestir its
imagination to consider what the whole exercise is in aid of, and
how best to elaborate changes which will intensify the significance of our historical progress. Before long the great debate is
resumed—and, behind it, mounting passions asserting that what
is at stake is so fundamental that no compromise can be considered. Once more, war knocks on the door.

A cheap and superficial reflection has often been made that although religions preach high moral standards, there is nothing more ruthless than wars of religion. More sensitively, Christian minds have been stunned to contemplate how it could be that the continent which cradled the young church and saw it grow to dominant maturity was the one in which warfare was indulged in with notorious constancy, culminating in the two disasters of this century. The perplexity is however lessened once it is realised that the basic religious preoccupation is with meaning before morals, and that while nothing can excuse the bloody inhumanities, the pretentious rivalries, the greed and flippancy which have marked European history at many points, the truly horrible wars were those in which, for good or ill, men believed that far more was at issue than their temporal advantage. In a tragic and ironic sense, the indescribable offences of the wars of religion and ideology were a perverse tribute to the conviction that there is something terribly important about getting right answers to ultimate questions.

It is easy to be supercilious about the earnestness and self-deception of other ages. But we would do well to reflect on the fact that our own age suffers some of its worst symptoms because men doubt whether life contains any worth while meaning at all. The neuroses of today are held by some to represent primarily the recoil from the pit of meaninglessness which so many see yawning at their feet. The apparently mindless excesses of teenage destructiveness and rejection must have their roots—in countries of many very different cultural, religious or ideological orthodoxies—in a sense that all these orthodoxies are basically phoney, pretty decorations on a gaping grave. At a higher level, the testimony of artists and musicians of our time is to a bare and austere economy of meaning appreciated with almost ascetic discipline. The terrible sense that we dare not let loose our ideological debate lest it break out once more into violence, coupled with the rapid social changes and uprooting which are the experiences of the young generation almost universally, create a situation where it is at once urgent and difficult to pursue the search for significance and reach some corporate articulation.

At such a moment it is hard to be invited blandly to accept ideological pluralism as a permanent condition. Men insist on meaning, and on meaning which is not simply subjective to themselves. They found it of old in religion, and there are those who entertain the hope that somehow everything can be put back comfortably to rights again if only religion will bestir itself and find the words and methods to offer to a new day the same service. The validity of this hope is the subject for further investigation in this chapter. But first we may note that as dogmatic, and intellectually serious, religious conviction has tended to evaporate, this has not led to general tolerance. Instead the locus of conviction has simply shifted elsewhere. 'You can believe what you like about the Holy Trinity, so long as you are sound on the Afro-Asian front' is the sarcastic remark of one who has watched the movement of attention, and noticed the seeds of the new intolerances. He might equally have identified the defenders of white civilisation as the new dogmatists if they had a more intellectually respectable case to support them. Either way, the battle for meaning is seen to be joined.

Now to return to the main issue in this chapter—the extent to which we may look to religion, or rather to the Christian tradition (which in this respect as in all else has very deep roots in Judaism), to provide for men the kind of understanding of life's meaning which will unite rather than divide. Can it answer, in its own way, the human insistence that our existence is worth enduring only if it signifies more than is immediately apparent? We are bound to begin this enquiry with two important reservations, and only in the light of them both will it be possible to make an affirmative assertion.

The first calls attention to the profound defence of agnosticism which is found in the Old Testament faith from the beginning. It is not at first easy to appreciate that this is a basic religious concern, when so many anxious teachers of Christianity spend their time affirming its certainties, to the neglect of some of the deepest notes in the concept of faith. But we can recall that from the start all the attempts on the part of the Jewish people to comprehend the being who, they believed, had addressed them were rebuffed. In the language forms of the day, God would not disclose his name. In the end, all that Moses could secure was apparently a word, the sense of which suggested a response to a cry for help and meant 'Here I am'. Such a name means everything or nothing. At the same time, God's people were forbidden expressly to make any visible respresentation of him. It is not always recognised what the real significance and consequence of this was. In that world the identification of divinity with certain material objects was common. In our more sophisticated times the things we venerate are less likely to be items of wood or stone so much as causes and intellectual constructions. But in both cases the principle is the same—that we ourselves are the architects of our own gods, and so can make them in shapes we find attractive, recognisable, and not too disturbing. That God is unrecognisable in simple terms was a lesson which the Jews had to learn the hard way, and which we theologians are always forgetting over again. The announcement of the Old Testament is that God knows his people, rather than that they know him. Indeed the whole length of it is the tale of their learning, and never knowing.

It might be protested that it was precisely this enforced agnosticism which was removed at the incarnation of Jesus Christ. Perhaps one of the great aberrations of the Western Christian tradition has been exactly this, the attempt to articulate a knowledge of God beyond our real range, and with our incredible intellectual apparatus, inherited from Greece and Rome, to delineate more than we could properly apprehend. This indeed may be one of the chief elements in the absorbing crisis of our day, as men start afresh to try to formulate the Christian faith. For we are finding it necessary to cast aside a too assertive knowledge of Jesus Christ himself, to return to the hard pilgrim's road of a very serious agnosticism, and to value afresh the commitment of faith outside the reach of assured knowledge. We are discovering that if Jesus Christ is for all men, this is not simply a wide and gracious universalism of concern, but it means also that there is no special life-raft of security provided for those of us who take his name——we must learn to swim with the rest. And what he has disclosed is above all the terms of a relationship rather than the face of God. No man has seen God at any time, a fact which the New Testament itself asserts, and such apprehension of him as we have, seen in a glass darkly, is by way of a commitment of faith rather than of incontrovertible logic or knowledge. The New Testament proclaims the possibility of a more intimate and reconciled relationship than ever before was dreamed of, without dispersing the mystery of him whose thoughts are not ours, nor his ways our ways. God's purpose, providing what meaning human life possesses, remains in large measure hidden. We are in fact invited to an act of trust: that the meaning which we do not see, except in broadest outline, is one which answers the deepest needs of our being. This degree of agnosticism is not a falling away from Christian faith, but rather a requirement of it.

Of course reverence for the mystery of God—and even acknowledgement that it is our estrangement which puts us in the position where of ourselves we cannot see—does not forbid the effort to put into coherent words and thought what we can rationally assemble of our intimations of the truth. This task of theology is a never-ending response of the human mind, which is not only permissible, but obligatory, if we are to try seriously to understand our faith as truth. But the provisional, tentative nature of our intellectual constructions has to be recognised from the start. And it may be that the real key to the ecumenical explosion of our day is just this discovery—forced upon us by the shattering effect on static types of thought systems caused by the speed of modern developments in extending human experience. Now we need companions in the search for truth far more than we need agreed paradigms from the denominational past.

The second important reservation is in a measure simply an intensification of the first. The Judaeo-Christian tradition has always clearly understood that familiarity with the thoughts of God is inaccessible to men, the works of his hand. So it has insisted that while human life and history have profound and ultimate meaning, the secret of that meaning is not precisely known to us but will appear only 'at the end'. But the Christian tradition itself has gone further. For the story of Jesus Christ is very much a tale of how he disowned or radically recast the hopes and meanings which the Jewish people had been taught to cherish as very much part of their understanding of

God. The source of that bitter hostility which ended in their crucifying him was just this, that he refused to accept their interpretation of historical meaning, and the meaning to which he committed himself on the cross was a scandal to them. The event itself, when understood in the light of the whole New Testament, did not disclose a Jewish responsibility for deicide, but a human alienation whereby even the people of God could wholly misunderstand their destiny. What Jesus did seemed incomprehensible even to his disciples, whom he had tried to prepare with every recollection of the hints and intimations of the past which he could bring to their minds. The rest of the Jewish people were even more in the dark, nor did the wisdom of the Greeks of that day provide a clue. For men, then as now, find it hardly possible to credit that their alienation from the true reality is so severe that a procedure called repentance is needed before they can begin to readjust their vision.

It is only in the light of this discovery that we can understand rightly the tragic quality of history without despair, the ever-renewed experience that in the very pursuit of meaning we destroy meaning, that the worst wars are those for the best causes, and that in our crippled hands love itself can be a suffocation. This is the deep reason why it becomes a certain Christian duty to demythologize politics and call in question the too assertive righteousness of those who strive for man's highest good. For we have before us all the time the symbol representing for ever the truth of our condition, that the only real meaning there is in human life is by us for ever being rejected, and that our hope lies in the incredible response to that rejection rather than in our achieving, one day, through the progressive evolution of the race, some kind of human perfection.

So there are two assertions about the meaning of human existence made in the Christian tradition. The first is the great affirmative that there is eternal significance for persons in the events and choices of history, that this is no cyclical tale of vanity, that the drama is real and the consequences of our decisions fateful, and that the process itself is a movement towards a culmination and consummation. This assertion gives meaning to the events of the moment but also insists that the fulness of meaning is yet to be disclosed. It therefore has evolutionary affinities, but with a difference. For the process is not just the gradual unfolding of what is already there, in the very nature of our human existence on earth. It is conceived, at least equally, to be a movement of separation—separating what is already there into clearer categories of good and evil—and the final justification of what is good.

The second assertion is related—that the meaning of human history, which we are called upon to believe as real, is nevertheless not in our possession, but can only be glimpsed rather than grasped. Properly speaking, therefore, Christianity ought never to find itself in conflict as one ideology with another (though we are always falling into this trap), but only with the pretensions of any ideology to possess the meaning of life. Too often Christianity has been presented as a brave antagonist of communist ideology in terms which simply identified Christianity with the ideologies of Western democracies. In fact, so long as Marxism offers to unveil the mechanics of social and economic power it must be taken seriously and judged simply by whether or not its account corresponds with the experience of life which we possess. No doubt it will be found to represent a great historical step in man's self-understanding, belonging to its day which was the middle part of the nineteenth century. It is only when it presents itself, not as a contribution to understanding social and economic mechanics, but as a complete and exhaustive account of meaning that we are bound to oppose it. But then we should be bound to oppose much else which overtly or covertly makes the same pretentious claims, whether it be in the name of 'Christian white civilisation' or the 'free society' or even 'emerging forces'.

Here we see the significance for world peace of something which at first appears completely unrelated to the hard realities of daily political decision. It is difficult to believe that the weekly activity of a small fragment of the human race in attending and participating in public worship in church has more than a very marginal importance in the struggle of mankind to avoid the nuclear holocaust. But this may be more because the forms of worship have been allowed to fall into anachronistic disrepair, so that men no longer are aware of what they are doing, than because the activity is intrinsically irrelevant. For the human search for meaning, which we have understood as unavoidable, is basically the search for the object of their admiration and devotion, which is what worship is about. The danger arises when men become convinced that they hold in their possession the fulness of meaning, and are thereby obliged to bring others into conformity. But true worship, as presented in the Christian tradition, begins with an acknowledgement of our own blindness, and looks to one who is not ourselves writ large, who is both our judge and creator, who is the meaning of our lives and yet with whom we are not simply identified—except by his grace in giving us forgiveness. This act of public worship affirms to the community at large that there is a meaning to our lives, but also that it is a meaning which is beyond and ahead, not in our grasp. Few human activities are more important for the peace of the world than that we should approach nations and cultures of apparently opposed character, not to present them with an ultimatum of conformity to our standards, but to search with them the unsearchable riches still beyond our reach. In this respect liturgical reform and the discovery of means of truly ecumenical worship may be one of the greatest contributions of the Christian community from its own resources to the world's safety.

It has been necessary thus to stress the relativities of our perception because we are so easily beguiled into accepting a view of the world which lacks the dimension of agnosticism. Once however this context has been established it is valid to make some more positive affirmations. If the whole meaning of the human story is not in our possession, at least we have certain highly important glimpses into its nature. And we can recognise at any rate that which tends to meaninglessness. We can commit ourselves to those objectives which keep open man's pilgrimage to a fuller apprehension of life's significance, and reject that which would prematurely foreclose it. But we can do more. We can describe with some assurance in what direction the search should lie. This is best done in terms of an earlier chapter. In Chapter II we investigated a method of moral judgement in terms of our relation and response to reality. If we follow the same clue now we can plot out some guide-lines for assessing which political developments threaten and which promise to enhance the life of men. The clues can be discovered by asking first what is the reality to which we are responding? And then we must inquire further about ourselves—who are we who do the responding?

In Chapter III we have already indicated broadly how within the Christian tradition we believe the human race is addressed by God in whom all our life is lived. We isolated three aspects of the matter. There is first the life-giving, life-affirming, where we speak of God giving us existence in the first place, and his thrusting us forward to more complex, responsible existence. This is something different from mere vitality, for the very definition of 'life' is made by one who at the crucial moment surrendered his life on earth for loyalty to something beyond it. But it is not at all a rejection of vitality in principle, very far from it. It is simply an indication that this is not the whole story, and that full life is more than vitality and may even conflict with it, at certain critical points. Our search for meaning in our human existence must therefore reflect this true humanism, which affirms the value of our earthly existence, its vitalities, its power, its enlargement, and must rejoice at every opportunity to make available to men increased possibilities of choice and activity. (Conversely, complacent acceptance of the lot of the poor, nations and social groups, is of itself a vote for the meaninglessness of life, and a rejection of what we believe to be the initiative of God to all men.) But the important and characteristic point about this attitude is that we are not thereby committed to a simple optimism about its outcome. This is to probe too far into the meaning of things, beyond our capacity. There is no suggestion in it that, once men have been relieved of the frustrations of life imposed by subjection to nature or to one another, they will find it easy to solve their conflicts and attain to all other virtues. This is not the lesson to be learned from our faith. It is rather that the risks involved in giving life to creatures like us have been accepted, and still the gift of life is continued. The consequences, according to the Christian story, are likely to be immense and even tragic, and still that is not the end of the matter. Our devotion to the cause of seeking liberty for subject peoples, economic development for developing countries, participation in the world's councils for those even who claim to be our enemies, is not a starry eyed optimism that men will thereby conveniently find the way to tranquillity and harmony. That would be to pursue our assertion of meaning beyond our competence. Instead we take the risks with eyes wide open—in the conviction that since God treats men in this way, there is ultimately no other option for us in our relations with one another. And just as we are aware in some measure of what the consequences are for God, represented in the symbol of the Cross, so we can be under no illusion that this too may be the price in human terms of the gift of life to men.

The second aspect of the divine address to the human race that we referred to, as part of the Christian tradition, is represented by the biblical concept of God speaking to men as equals. We referred there to the assumption, so complete as to pass unnoticed, that God did not compel men's response, but in a hiddenness which alone made possible a conversation, sought to preserve at any cost men's capacity to originate their own reply. We pointed out the implications of this to the whole cause of civil and religious liberty. Traditionally we debate this question under the title of 'freedom'. But it is a word of very uncertain meaning, with strong emotional associations obscuring the many ambiguities it contains. Naturally all of us welcome the thought of being in some way released from the frustrations of our lives, becoming masters of our environment, and, perhaps even more, of opposing human wills. The battle-cry of freedom is always assured of a ready response. But it must always be, in reality, a very relative experience if our lives are conceived in terms of response. The greatest liberty we can have is then derived from a full understanding and acceptance of the reality—natural, divine or human—with which we have to deal, so that we can make the response appropriate to such a situation. In this respect Marx was right to repeat that freedom is the recognition of necessity. It is only when we realise that the reality with which we are dealing is both personal, and addresses us with the words of conversation, that the necessity itself begins to carry a deeper meaning.

It is even more difficult to define the idea of freedom in political terms. For the whole apparatus of politics and government, whatever its advocates say, is an essay in how to control widely divergent wills and purposes so that they are not mutually frustrating. Inevitably it is an essay in limiting freedom in some degree. Moreover, as the direction of modern complex societies becomes more and more a highly technical affair, it cannot really be pretended that a nation's business is effectively transacted by some development of the old village moot, where everyone, or at least everyone's representative, had a say in arriving at decisions.

For our purposes, therefore, another way of approaching the matter is preferable. It is the recognition that each human being is a genuine originator of responses to reality, to an extent which varies widely but which is the distinguishing mark of humanity itself. Our concern here must be that the originality and creativity of men should be fostered rather than suppressed, most especially in their discernment of meaning in human life. Much of our lives has been, and will be, determined by the decisions of others and by the pressures of things and events over which we have little control. But the shape of any tolerable world-society must be such that it safeguards a man's responsibility to make his own answer to the challenge of life, at the deepest level. The witness he feels bound to bear to what life is all about must be allowed to be not only free but audible elsewhere as a contribution to the whole human debate. Once again, this is not because all our discernment is of value, or that there is any guarantee that men will use this capacity for their own or the common good. It is to be distinguished from liberation philosophies which proclaim what we cannot know but may reasonably, on the existing evidence, doubt. It is rather the inevitable deduction from the faith that God treats us in this way, and takes the consequences, and we have no option but to do likewise.

This is the argument for recognising the international struggle to arrive at enforceable standards of human rights and religious liberty as an essential pre-requisite for the building of a world-society capable of maintaining peace. But so long as the battle is conceived in individualistic terms some of the most difficult issues are obscured. For what is at stake is not simply the right of the non-conforming individual to be himself over against the political and social pressures upon him. There is also the question how far public institutions should reflect any particular view of the meaning of life, or should be controlled by an ideological or religious (or anti-religious) philosophy. Indeed the question is even more whether public institutions can in reality be neutral. They can intend to be so, and on first sight they may appear to be uncommitted. But in fact a system of public education, the state's support of the arts or control of public entertainment, even a library service, will manifest principles of selection and sets of assumptions—perhaps the more influential when they are least consciously formulated. The nation most aware of its character as a secular, uncommitted state may turn out the most prone to nationalistic or cultural self-satisfaction, in so far as, lacking any other principle of unification, it makes the most of unities which are to be found latent in its existing conditions.

The moral of this is, not to intensify the effort to be un-committed. Rather it is deliberately to arrange that those who contend within the secular state for the right to contribute their view about the meaning of the nation's life are given full oppor-tunity to do so, in competition with each other. Meanwhile the state itself deliberately restrains itself, and is restrained by such arrangements, from giving more than provisional validity to such national consensus as it may represent. The choice, for in-stance, is not between an educational system which excludes religious considerations (such a system would already be pre-judiced in one direction, at least to the extent of indicating that one can come to terms with all the necessary truths for life with-out ever raising a serious religious question), and one which is ideologically or religiously controlled. There is quite another possibility. This is an educational system conscious of the assumptions which it finds necessary in order to get into action at all; aware of the provisional nature of such assumptions; and deliberately making room at the appropriate level within the system for the critique of its assumptions from various angles, representing the plurality of serious conviction within the nation. In such a context, religious freedom is not seen as the exclusion of the religious question from consideration in the con-struction of public institutions, but rather as the recognition that the religious questions must not be taken as answered and closed but regarded as a vital point of growth in a society. It is only in this kind of pattern that one can properly consider the emergence of a world society, amongst peoples so varied in their religious inheritance. The easy way out is to imagine the super-cession of all divisive religions by one modern type of secular humanism. But if the argument of this chapter is valid, such a development would represent a wholly premature effort to close the discussion, would contain the seeds of a very oppressive totalitarianism of the mind, and would at once block the road to an understanding of the mystery and meaning of life fuller than is yet imaginable. For these and other reasons such an attempt to fix the future would surely soon be seen as conserva-tive and reactionary rather than liberating.

Already we have approached the second of our sources of clues —the question asked of the Christian tradition, not regarding the reality to which we are responding, but who we are who respond. In a sense the question is already largely answered in what has gone before. We are those who are considered worth addressing in a certain way, as though our own response was of the highest significance. This emphasis on human dignity is the basic assertion of the biblical tradition, however much theo-logians may have tended to harp on its qualification about human sin. Indeed the one excellent reason for turning once again, in this particular political context, to the negative assess-ment is as a safeguard, so that human nature may realise its true value. The case is best made out in concrete terms rather than in general assertions about human nature and its mythical past in the Garden of Eden. We can confine ourselves to familiar facts of experience. We are aware, for instance, that our own claims on life are always more vividly before our minds than the needs of others, and that it is natural for us to tend to exaggerate what is justly due to ourselves and to underestimate the proper demands of others. The one comes naturally, the other only with con-scious effort. At a more developed level, we give primacy to our own understanding of the good, and this is always infected be-cause of our unwillingness to be disturbed. More threatening to others is our inevitable insistence on having our own way, if possible—having convinced ourselves that this way is generally beneficial. All of this is the routine of political calculation, the stuff out of which common action has to be fashioned. It is not by any means a complete account of human motivation, but although individuals may transcend these limitations, social and political groups find they have to seek their common denominator for action at the lower rather than the higher end of the scale.

For our present purposes, the significance of a realistic appreciation of man's alienation from the true roots of his being (of which all these characteristics are symptoms) is this. It is a warning of the dangers of that kind of ideological or idealistic assumption which tends to utopianism in thought, and to the neglect of those safeguards against the oppression of the weak by the powerful which tends to be its practical expression. A recognition of the destructive and 'imperialist' strain in human society is not suggested in order to down-grade the human race but in order to protect it from itself. This kind of Christian realism is possible once men accept a judgement of themselves and human history from beyond man and history themselves, and this in turn is only tolerable when the judgement they must face is intimately associated with the promise of forgiveness for those who are prepared to endure their moment of truth.

Some at least of the political philosophy of the West has been imbued with this perception, so that while power has been accepted and developed, those with access to it have been hedged around with careful limitations. But too easily it has been imagined that the particular system of safeguards elaborated in the Western parliamentary tradition were necessarily the best or the only way of giving political recognition to this view of the human situation. Other nations and cultures (including those of the new developing world), finding the particular parliamentary forms they inherited from the West uncongenial, have not always appreciated the need to devise their own methods for achieving the same necessary result—the control of the human exploitation of power. But in any project for going beyond our present balkanised world to some system giving hope for a measure of tolerable universal order, full account will have to be taken of this realistic aspect of human organisation. Whether it be in some development of the United Nations; or the growth of regional systems, after the pattern attempted in Western Europe, which in turn come to terms with each other; or whether in some other way—it will be necessary to balance power with power. It will be necessary to discern, beneath the formal legal patterns we elaborate in our constitutional arrangements, what groups of men, interests and organisations, are in fact going to be substantially decisive, and therefore how they can be made to act responsibly. We have so to create order that at the same time we deflect the possibility of tyranny and exploitation.

Once more the provisional and incomplete aspect of human history presents itself. All our solutions are partial, contingent and temporary, a balance of advantages carefully struck and constantly reviewed. None, in the Christian view, can represent the final meaning of our lives on earth. Indeed the greatest threat to human life in history perceived in the Jewish-Christian tradition is that involved in the attempt to find ultimate meaning in our political and social structures. This is the idolatry which in the end demands human sacrifice, the liquidation of men on the altar of ideology. We know this all too well in the twentieth century.

But if there is no political and social structure which can contain the meaning of our lives, there are certainly some which can betray and distort that meaning as we already recognise, and some which can create conditions in which our understanding of life's meaning can be enriched and enlarged. It is therefore one of the great functions of true religion in the political realm to present at every point a determined challenge to all absolutising of political philosophies and programmes, to expose the relative and provisional character of all political choices, and at the same time, with equal and even greater vigour, to provide the stimulus and conviction for men to pursue what is good in what is partial, temporary, and always incomplete. Religious sophistication is a dedication to that which is always beyond our apprehension in the terms of our life on this planet.

INDEX

Abraham, 57
Acton, Lord, 95
Ahaz, 61
Amos, 61

Balance of power, 28 ff.
Baring, Sir Evelyn, 18, 19
Bloch, Ernest, 98
Bonhoeffer, Dietrich, 47, 101 ff.
Butterfield, Herbert, 46
Byzantine theology, 101

Capitalism, 20 ff., 116
Capitalist states, 20 ff., 116
Charles V, 34
Churchill, Winston, 9, 29, 62
Cobden, Richard, 29
Corbett, Patrick, 115
Cox, Harvey, 98

Dark Ages, 30
De Tocqueville, 121
Democracy, 23
Disarmament, 79 ff., 91, 92
Dodd, C. H., 65
Dubois, Pierre, 30, 31

Eisenhower, Dwight, 24
European Economic Community,
  25, 49
European Enlightenment, 84

First World War, 29
Francis I, 34

Frankel, Charles, 95
Freedom, 46, 135
French Revolution, 21
Freud, Sigmund, 93

Galileo, 54
Gospel, 63 ff.

Hegel, G. W. F., 93-94
History, 105 ff.
Hitler, Adolf, 34
Howard, Michael, 34

Ideologies, 115 ff.
Imperialism, 20 ff., 28
Industrial Revolution, 24
Isaiah, 61

Jeremiah, 61
Jesus Christ, 55, 58, 63 ff., 71, 98 ff.,
  129 f.
Job, 74
Just War, 70

Kant, Immanuel, 50
Kennedy, J. F., 24

Law, 119 ff.
League of Nations, 30
Leibnitz, G. W., 24

Manchester School, 88
Marx, Marxism, 23-24, 48, 76-77,
  80, 83, 93 ff., 116, 132, 135

Manson, T. W., 65
Mazzini, Giuseppe, 22
McNamara, Robert, 24
Mead, Margaret, 16
Mill, James, 21
Milne, A. A., 29-30
Milner, Lord, 18
Moral judgment, 38-46, 53
Morality, 119 ff.
Moses, Law of, 55 ff., 129

Nationalism, 35-36
Niebuhr, Richard, 46 ff.
Nuclear weapons, 91

Oliver, F. S., 19

Paine, Thomas, 21
Paul, 99-100
Penn, William, 31
Pharisees, 60
Picasso, 7
Plato, 50, 95

Progress, progressive, 82 ff.
Prophets, 59 ff.

Reformation, 30
Relationship, 66 ff.
Renaissance, 101
Responsibility, 46 ff.
Richardson, Alan, 55
Rosinski, Herbert, 76, 80
Rousseau, J. J., 27

Second World War, 35, 45
Sully, 31

Tawney, R. H., 23

United Nations, 22, 30, 112, 123-5
UNCTAD, 125
UNESCO, 15, 17
UN Secretariat, 125

Waltz, Kenneth, 15
Whitehouse, W. A., 55, 58